The
Shotgunner's
Bible

THE SHOTGUNNER'S BIBLE

George Laycock

DOUBLEDAY & COMPANY, INC., GARDEN CITY, NEW YORK •

ISBN: 0-385-00978-X
Library of Congress Catalog Card Number 69–15216
Copyright © 1969 by George Laycock
Printed in the United States of America
9 8 7 6 5

CONTENTS

The
Shotgunner's
Bible

Chapter 1

THE VERSATILE SHOTGUN

On a clear frosty morning two men with their dogs left the car at the roadside and started across the open fields. Suddenly, near the weedy fencerow marking the field's boundary, the first of the dogs skidded to a halt and posed rigidly with her nose pointed into a tangle of briars and saplings. Her entire body was at attention.

By now the second dog, a few paces behind and slightly to one side, was also on rigid point. The two hunters quickly moved in. One of them stepped past the dogs and kicked the thick-growing brush.

With a pounding of brown wings, a large bird bounded from the thicket, and a dozen feet above the ground wheeled in a ninety-degree turn to hurtle toward a woodlot across three hundred yards of open plowed field. Both guns swung up and followed, but there was no shot. "Hen bird," the first hunter called, and both guns were lowered.

As they bent down to pet and praise their dogs, there rose from almost beneath their feet, a cackling, brilliantly hued cock pheasant. He cleared the weed tops, stayed low, and gathered speed as he headed for the woods.

The startled hunters recovered their wits, and swung in unison on the big cackling bird. The first gun spoke and missed. The follow-up from the other gun scored, and the dogs raced forward to retrieve the bird.

Across America, in any autumn, the scene is duplicated thousands of times as some ten million shotgun owners tramp the open fields.

Over the years, the shotgun has enriched American tradition, and become a cherished link with an age when man obtained his food by virtue of his hunting abilities and his marksmanship. The lure of the hunting fields is still strong. According to recent figures, more than 84 percent of the hunting licenses purchased in this country are bought by shotgun carriers. The shotgun provides recreation the year around because it is the world's most versatile gun. For the average man, woman, or child, it is also the biggest value for the gun-purchaser's dollar.

Millions of shotgun owners know they can utilize the same gun for hunting ducks, pheasants, rabbits, squirrels, pursuing grouse, quail, woodcock and, with the proper ammunition, even geese and deer.

Game seasons run through several months in fall and winter. Licensed shooting preserves are often open six months or more of each year. The year around, gun clubs provide regular shooting at clay targets. Someone once figured that in Ohio alone, shotgunners shoot at 183 million clay targets a year, most of them at small trap ranges around the state. Someone else with a sense of arithmetic—or the ridiculous—calculated that, placed end to end, these targets would reach more than halfway around the world, which, while perhaps true, would certainly be an inconvenience for the trap boys.

By definition, the shotgun is a smoothbore. Typically, but not universally, it fires many lead pellets at one time. These pellets form a pattern of shot which accounts for the gun's effectiveness in shooting fast-moving targets.

Shotguns are essentially short-range guns. As the charge of shot travels away from the gun it spreads in an ever-widening pattern and loses velocity rapidly.

Of the ammunitions commonly marketed for shotguns the 12-gauge rifled slug is likely to travel farthest. One ballistics formula for computing ranges places the maximum distance for a 12-gauge slug at 1420 yards, the maximum distance for No. 6 shot at 242 yards, and for No. 9 shot at 176 yards. Such figures, however, give an exaggerated impression of the effective range of shotgun ammunition. Most shots are taken at distances under fifty yards, and effective shots can scarcely ever be expected at ranges of seventy-five yards or more, except perhaps in some cases with rifled slugs.

Shotguns are limited less by the size of the game than by the distance from the hunter. They have been effectively used on all sizes of game, including elephants, providing the hunter was daring enough to get within range. Sir Samuel Baker, famed explorer of the Nile Valley who discovered, among other wonders, Murchison Falls, shot elephants with four-bore, and even two-bore shotguns. The barrel of the four-bore would accommodate a lead ball weighing a quarter of a

Shotgun sports are an excellent way for fathers to go afield with their boys and instill in them a love of the outdoors as well as the basic elements of good gun handling. *By Savage Arms.*

pound, and the rare two-bore gun called for a projectile that weighed half a pound. But Sir Samuel spoke of approaching the tail of the elephants so close he could have touched them with his gun.

There are practical limits to the sizes of shotguns. In the 1800s the 10-gauge shotgun was rather commonly used on waterfowl. But today most shotgunners are willing to settle for a 12-gauge. Loaded with modern magnum ammunition, the 12-gauge will accomplish practically anything the old 10 might have done. The smallest production model shotgun is the .410, a satisfactory lightweight gun for shooting small game at short range or for the expert on the skeet range. Within these limits—12-gauge to .410 caliber—fall practically all the modern shotguns manufactured. If much larger they become too heavy to

The versatile shotgun is useful on inanimate targets as well as live game. Here Hart Luebkeman uses a mechanical trap to throw clay targets for his father, George, in a farmer's field near their Cincinnati home. *By George Laycock.*

be pleasant for shooting, and below the .410 they are too small to be effective.

Old records reveal that the earliest shotgun in this country probably came in with Christopher Columbus. Since that time they have been carried, and used, by both the good guys and the bad. Western stagecoach guards preferred them because of the wide pattern of shot they would spray from a bouncing wagon seat. Weddings were sanctified with shotguns, duels were fought with them and robberies committed, and thwarted, with them.

Men often develop lasting fondness for a shotgun they have carried over the years. In Oklahoma an aging hunter recently pointed out that he had not missed a regular hunting day in the quail season in thirty-five years, and he had carried the same shotgun for fifty-three years. The gun originally cost him fifteen dollars. In 1925 and again in 1932, he had stored his hunting licenses in the stock. This turned out to have unexpected benefits.

Eventually he decided to apply for Social Security, but fire had destroyed all records of his age. He picked up his aging shotgun, determined

Increasingly popular with bird hunters is the autoloading shotgun such as this 12-gauge with ventilated rib. *By George Laycock.*

This collection of illegal guns is typical of the destructive weapons once used by waterfowl market hunters. These guns were confiscated by government agents. *By U. S. Fish and Wildlife Service.*

to go hunt a few birds, and forget his troubles. It was then he remembered the old licenses hidden in its stock. They provided proof of his age. Some of the Social Security payments doubtless went toward the purchase of new shells. But the old gun was good enough.

As Thomas Hall, curator of the Winchester Gun Museum in New Haven, Connecticut, has pointed out, the ancestor of the modern shotgun came into the picture while the landed gentry and nobility of Europe still amused themselves chasing game with falcons, or riding to the hounds. Considering the earliest of the shotguns, this may be understandable. The first ancestors of the modern shotgun were crude hand cannons designed for use in battle. In use by 1350, small and lightweight enough for one man to handle, these were brass or iron tubes, with a closed end, fire hole,

This shotgun-carrying bobcat hunter brings in a day's catch, taken with the aid of his hound. *By George Laycock.*

and wooden stock—clumsy, noisy, dirty, inaccurate—but promising.

Sometime before the seventeenth century these guns had been adapted to the hunting of small game, especially birds, not for sport, but for the meat it yielded. The guns were more effective against birds at rest than on the wing.

The upper classes left bird shooting to the poor folks. Then in the latter half of the 1600s the noblemen decided that whatever the peasantry was up to out there in the coverts with their fowling pieces, might be proper fun, so they began to take up the fowling pieces for their own pleasure. From then on, the shotgun sports were on the ascendancy. With this growing interest came a series of improvements that by the latter part of the 1700s brought shotguns up to approximately their modern appearance.

Early fowling pieces, in use during the second half of the sixteenth century, were usually matchlocks. As Tom Hall points out from his long study of firearms, "They had short curved stocks and long barrels 40 to 50 inches in length." For many years there was not to be much basic difference between military guns and those made primarily for fowling pieces. The long barrels and heavy stocks made such guns slow to handle compared with today's sleek, lightweight shotguns.

The flintlock, it is believed, was invented about 1615. It ignited powder by striking into it a spark from a flint. The earliest shot were little pieces of lead, cut instead of cast in spherical form as shot is today. After the development of shotgun shells early in the 1870s, the old muzzleloaders were doomed to give way rapidly to breech-loading shotguns.

Among the unusual shotguns of the past was the blunderbuss with its funnel-shaped muzzle resembling an old-fashioned hearing aid. Into the muzzle of these frightening devices would go a generous helping of black powder followed by a wad, then a collection of shot, perhaps other hard objects handy and small enough to rattle down into the tube, and then another wad. At close range the blunderbuss was capable of scaring the devil out of any unfortunate caught in

One of the reasons for carrying a shotgun on African safari is to try for the native sand grouse that come to the watering holes late in the day. *By Erwin A. Bauer.*

This Merkel 20-gauge over-and-under, with Kersten fastening and fast-selecting single trigger, is a favorite field gun for upland game for George Luebkeman of Cincinnati. The fine engraving adds to its value and makes the shotgun a cherished possession. *By George Laycock.*

The shotgun did its work for this fox hunter who was waiting at a crossing when his dogs brought the game into range. *By Erwin A. Bauer.*

front of it, and most of those to the side or rear as well. It is quite likely that its greatest power was psychological, although it could, and did, deliver mortal blows to assorted creatures including rafts of sitting ducks when the gunner was lucky enough to get close to them.

Market hunters, before laws were passed to protect waterfowl from slaughter, developed huge punt guns. They were so named because they were carried in shallow-draft punt boats which were eased in close to rafts of ducks. Some of the biggest punt guns weighed as much as one hundred pounds, had barrels nine feet long, and shot two pounds or more of shot at a blast. Fired upon sitting or rising ducks, they might bring down seventy-five or a hundred ducks in a single shot.

Old-time whalers, seeking better ways to subdue the giants of the seas, turned to the shotguns of the times and adapted the idea to firing a lance from a shoulder gun that might weigh twenty pounds and which would more than likely

Here is a typical autumn harvest scene in which the Browning over-and-under is a traditional element. *By Erwin A. Bauer.*

roll the gunner backward across the deck.

During World War II shotguns played a major role in the Air Force, not as armament but as part of the training equipment for aerial gunners. Many of the country's finest shotgun marksmen, once called away from the trap and skeet fields for military service, were assigned duty as Air Force gunnery instructors. They began not with rifles and machine guns, but with shotguns.

Using shotguns, the trainee learned how to lead a target while shooting from a moving vehicle. Airplane turrets were mounted on trucks so gunners revolving in turrets could practice on targets thrown from skeet towers. At least one such training center had a half-mile oval track around which trucks drove while students in revolving chairs shot so fast they scarcely had time to reload.

But these are the specialized uses of the shotgun, the exceptions which prove its versatility. This historic firearm has its major role, from day to day and year to year, in the hands of millions of hunters and target shooters. Shotgun owners everywhere can find added pleasure in the study of their guns, and most can find increased satisfaction from more skillful shooting.

For practice and fun the hunter and his partner can take turns throwing targets for each other if the live game should be in short supply. *By Erwin A. Bauer.*

Chapter 2

TYPES OF SHOTGUNS

Classified according to the kind of action they employ, shotguns can be separted into the break-open designs, bolt action, lever action, pump guns and autoloaders. Which one a person selects depends on what he wants the gun to do for him, how much he can spend on it, and, in many instances, certain prejudices for and against various types of guns.

BREAK OPEN

Side-by-Side Doubles

The earliest shotguns I remember, and the kind my father always had around the farm at home, were double-barrel, side-by-side break-open instruments. Eventually I learned that shotguns came in other styles, but the old double-barrel was then the most popular member of the shotgun family, and it is still highly popular. Chances are good that it would be even more so if the handwork required in its manufacture had not increased its relative price and put it in a weaker competitive position with the repeater types.

Evidence that American gunners have never forgotten nor forsaken the double is the return by Marlin in recent times of the famed old L. C. Smith, one of the all-time favorites. The gunsmiths who had once made these doubles were gone. But Marlin still had the original plans as a guide. Most doubles, offered today, however, are foreign-made guns.

The double gun breaks open in a manner that enables the shooter to look easily through the barrels for obstructions such as snow or mud. When open, the chambers and shells are in full view, which makes it easy to see if the gun is loaded. As long as it is open it cannot fire, which gives the break-open gun a positive safety margin.

Other models enable the shooter to keep more shells in the gun, but in upland hunting two shots are usually as many as a person can fire before the game is out of range. Many waterfowl hunters want that third shell that is available with an autoloader or pump gun.

Some doubles give the shooter the advantage of barrels with different chokes. The first shot at a going-away target can be taken with the barrel providing the more open pattern, while the second barrel delivers a follow-up shot with more choke, when the game is presumably farther away.

Double-barrel shotguns may come equipped with either one or two triggers. The more expensive models are single-trigger guns. The best ones are equipped so the shooter can, by pressing a button, fire his choice of the right or left barrel first and not have them fire in a set order every time. They may be equipped with ejectors that kick the empties all the way out as the gun is opened, or with extractors, which make it necessary to remove fired shells by hand.

This lineup of three popular field guns includes, left to right, Winchester 12-gauge Magnum pump gun with a 1-X Weaver-Scope, Browning over-and-under double-barrel, Remington 870 pump gun with a 2-X Weaver-Scope. *By Erwin A. Bauer.*

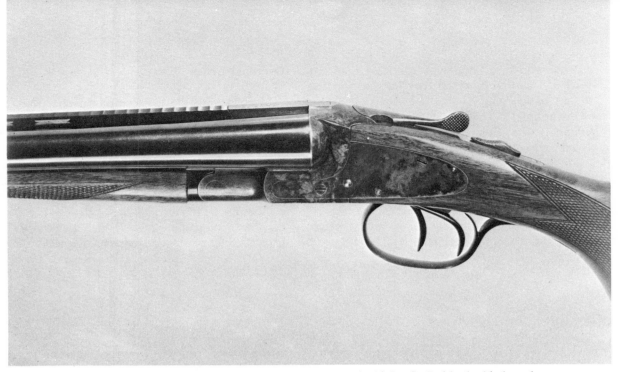

In 1967 Marlin Firearms brought back their famed old L. C. Smith double-barrel, shown here with the action closed. *By Marlin Firearms Co.*

Selection of typical field guns, starting upper left. Remington 870 pump with 2-X Weaver-Scope. Remington double-barrel 12-gauge. Remington Model 11-48 auto-loading 16-gauge. Remington Model 1100 autoloader with ventilated rib 12-gauge. *By George Laycock.*

Those who favor side-by-side doubles like the speed and ease with which they handle, and the balance of the gun.

One unusual double which is not a break-open design, is the French-made Darne. Now imported and sold in the United States, it employs a sliding breech-type action. The Darne sliding action has been manufactured since the late 1800s. It is said to be rugged, dependable, and well balanced. But, like other doubles, it is manufactured with much handwork, a factor which adds to the price. It is available in 12-, 20-, and 28-gauge.

Over-and-Under

Doubles with the tubes arranged one over the other offer the advantage of two barrels but a single barrel over which to sight. For some gun handlers, this works out better than sighting down the space between two barrels. Popularity of the over-and-under, compared with the side-by-side double, is growing. The over-and-under is often a good choice for the shooter who also shoots an autoloader or pump gun with their single barrels. It may be, however, that the single sighting plane feature is overrated. Many shooters get along just

One of the simplest styles of shotgun in use today is this two-piece model from the Philippines. The gun is loaded by placing a shell in the back end of the long piece of pipe. The shooter then gently inserts the pipe into the section that is fitted to the stock. When ready to shoot he pulls the barrel back in the fitting and the primer makes contact with a firing pin. *By George Laycock.*

as well with a side-by-side equipped with a ventilated rib. It is generally agreed that the over-and-under delivers less apparent recoil from the lower barrel than is felt from the side-by-side double. The explanation lies in the fact that the bottom barrel is in a straighter line from the shoulder. Because the bottom barrel has less choke and is consequently the first one fired on regular going-away shots, its softer apparent recoil lets a shooter hold better on his target for the second shot. This, however, can all be lost on the shooter to whom the over-and-under "just doesn't feel right."

Single-Barrel

The single-barrel break-open shotgun is about as basic as a shotgun can be. This type gun comes in two classifications, however, one low in price, the other not so low. The lowest-priced ones are often purchased as first shotguns for young shooters. The higher-priced single shots are made to meet the demanding requirements of the trap shooter. Long barrels, too long for most shooting, are typical of these trap guns. Some are thirty-six inches long. The added length is an advantage in pointing.

For the beginner, the biggest advantage of the single shot is its low cost. But with this type gun, also, the young shooter must learn to make his shots count. If he shoots at a bird and misses, there rarely is time to reload and fire a second shot. Many hunters of long experience still cherish warm memories of that first single-barrel gun. But it may well be that the memories of the gun get all mixed up with other elements of those wonderful days in the field. Today's youthful hunter carrying a 20-gauge autoloader will probably someday recall his boyhood hunting experiences just as warmly as those who started out with a single shot.

BOLT ACTION

Another type shotgun in the economy class is the bolt action. These are good, solid, dependable guns. They ordinarily carry extra shells in a magazine fitted into the breech in such a manner that the action of the bolt ejects the fired shell and loads the next one into the chamber.

But few shotgunners can ever hope to become fast enough to get off a second shot at a cackling cock pheasant or fleeting dove with a bolt-action shotgun. Except for the fact that it carries a supply of shells in a convenient location, the gun is little better than a single shot. It is slower to use than the almost extinct lever-action shotgun.

LEVER ACTION

Rarest of the shotgun types is the lever-action repeater. Oldtime models should be checked for size of the chamber in terms of modern ammunition. One 12-gauge made by Winchester and discontinued in 1901 was chambered for 2⅝-inch shells.

The lever-action gun is equipped with a lever in such a position that it serves also as the trigger guard. It is swung down to eject the fired shell and load the next one, an act which can be accomplished with considerable speed.

PUMP GUNS

Demonstrations by highly skilled shooters have shown that the pump gun can fire as fast as the autoloader, or could, at least, before the gas-operated autoloaders came along. But this has about as much application to rabbit hunting as a bikini to life in the Arctic. Both guns can be fast, but that is not the point on which they should be divided. Each has a lot going for it.

The pump gun, which ranks at or near the top today in shotgun popularity in the United States, is an economical gun to produce. Modern machine techniques can be applied neatly to its manufacture, which places it in the moderate-price range among shotguns considerably cheaper, generally speaking, than either the double or the autoloader.

In addition, a good pump gun is a rugged piece of equipment that the average shotgunner is unlikely to wear out during his own lifetime. The average gun, according to one manufacturer, fires about three thousand rounds in its lifetime. But one trap shooter returned his pump gun to the manufacturer after firing 226,397 rounds, and all it needed then was rebluing. Like other single-barrel shotguns, the pump gun can be fitted with variable choke devices, adding versatility for the one-gun man.

Pump guns are an American creation, tracing their development back to the Connecticut gun shop of Christopher Spencer. They were prominent on the market and in the hunting fields well before the turn of the present century. The

(text continues page 46)

Mossberg Model 183D, .410-gauge, three-shot, bolt action with interchangeable chokes. *By Mossberg.*

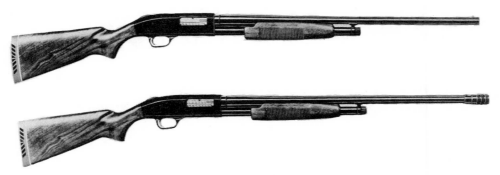

Mossberg Model 500 pump-action shotgun available in various gauges with interchangeable barrels and with or without choke device. *By Mossberg.*

Mossberg Model 390K bolt action, 16-gauge, three-shot with selective choke chambered for 2¾-inch shells, regular or Magnum. *By Mossberg.*

Mossberg Model 183K, .410-gauge, bolt action with selective choke. *By Mossberg.*

Mossberg Model 500 pump with ventilated rib and selective choke for Magnum or regular load. *By Mossberg.*

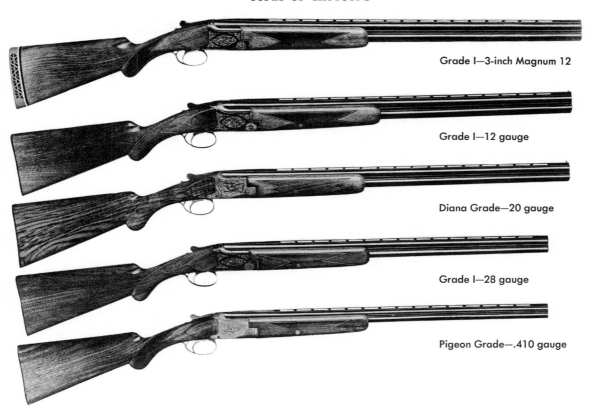

Grade I—3-inch Magnum 12

Grade I—12 gauge

Diana Grade—20 gauge

Grade I—28 gauge

Pigeon Grade—.410 gauge

Browning over-and-unders with ventilated rib. *By Browning Arms Co.*

Browning superposed trap model. *By Browning Arms Co.*

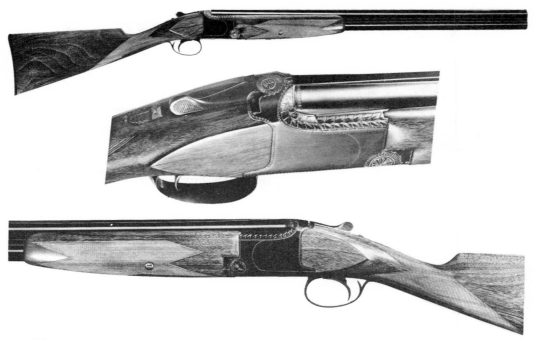

This Browning over-and-under is a lightweight field model. *By Browning Arms Co.*

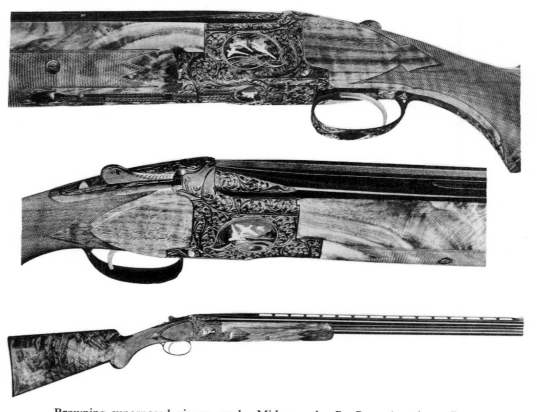

Browning superposed pigeon grade, Midas grade. *By Browning Arms Co.*

Browning autoloading 20-gauge for three-inch Magnum shells. *By Browning Arms Co.*

Four different models of the Browning over-and-under shotgun, top to bottom, trap model 12-gauge, three-inch Magnum 12-gauge, hunting and skeet 12-gauge, hunting and skeet 20-gauge. *By Browning Arms Co.*

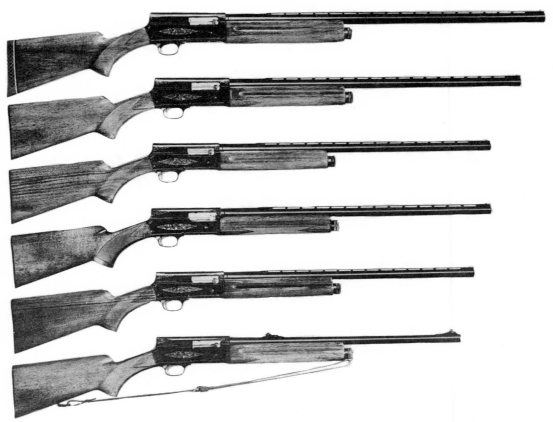

Browning automatic shotguns. Five-shot capacity except in guns chambering three-inch Magnums. Crossbolt safety. Top-to-bottom, 12-gauge three-inch Magnum, 12-gauge standard and lightweight, 16-gauge lightweight, 20-gauge three-inch Magnum, 20-gauge lightweight, and 12-gauge buck special made for rifled slug and buckshot loads. *By Browning Arms Co.*

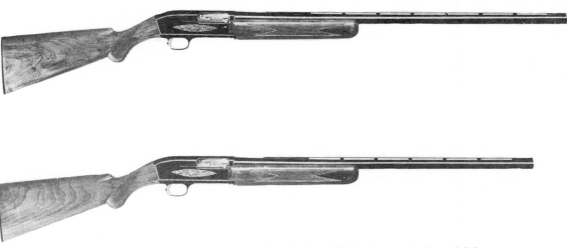

Browning double automatic shotguns chambering 2¾-inch standard and Magnum loads. *By Browning Arms Co.*

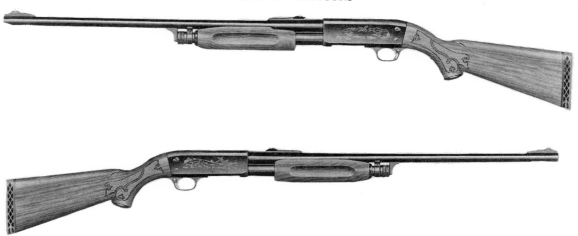

Ithaca Model 37 Deerslayer in 12-, 16-, and 20-gauges. *By Ithaca Gun Co.*

Same with leather sling and receiver peep sight. *By Ithaca Gun Co.*

Ithaca three-thousand-dollar trap gun, close-up showing engraving on receiver. Mostly hand-made. *By Ithaca Gun Co.*

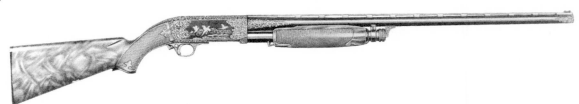

Ithaca Custom-Crafted three-thousand-dollar Grade Repeater with engraved receiver and 24K gold embossing, a custom-made shotgun. *By Ithaca Gun Co.*

Ithaca 4E grade single-barrel trap gun. *By Ithaca Gun Co.*

Ithaca 5E grade trap gun. *By Ithaca Gun Co.*

Ithaca SKB Model. Top to bottom: 100 grade side-by-side double, 200E grade side-by-side double, 500 grade over-and-under double, 600 field over-and-under double, 600 trap over-and-under double. *By Ithaca Gun Co.*

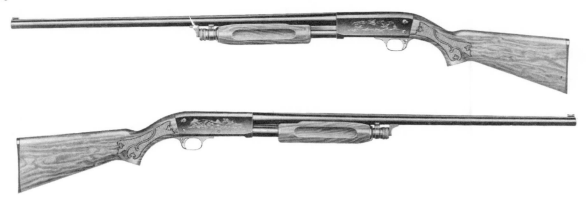

Ithaca Model 37R slide action. *By Ithaca Gun Co.*

Ithaca Model 37 Deerslayer with scope. *By Ithaca Gun Co.*

Ithaca Model 37 Featherlight Repeater, five-shell capacity, barrel in twenty-six, twenty-eight, or thirty-inch lengths. Bottom ejection. *By Ithaca Gun Co.*

Ithaca Model 37 with ventilated rib. *By Ithaca Gun Co.*

Ithaca Model 37D. *By Ithaca Gun Co.*

Coltsman standard pump shotgun. In 12-, 16-, and 20-gauges. *By Colt Firearms.*

Stevens Model 940, single-barrel side-lever in 12-, 16-, 20-, 28-, and .410-gauges. *By Savage Arms.*

Stevens Model 940Y in 20 and .410 with twenty-six-inch barrel. Shortened stock with recoil pad especially for younger shooters. *By Savage Arms.*

Fox Model B-SE in 12-, 16-, 20-, and .410-gauges. Hammerless double-barrel. Chambered for 2¾-inch shells, 20- and .410-gauge for three-inch shells. *By Savage Arms.*

Savage 750-AC. The Savage 750 fitted with adjustable choke. *By Savage Arms.*

Savage 750 chambered for 2¾-inch shells; 12-gauge. Improved cylinder in twenty-six-inch barrel, modified or full choke in twenty-eight-inch barrel. *By Savage Arms.*

Stevens 311, in 12-, 16-, 20- and .410-gauges, hammerless. *By Savage Arms.*

Savage 220-L. Hammerless single barrel in 12-, 16-, 20-, and .410-gauges. Chambers 2¾-inch shells, except .410-gauge, which chambers three-inch shells. *By Savage Arms.*

Stevens 95. 12-gauge single-barrel chambered for 2¾- or three-inch shells. *By Savage Arms.*

Stevens 94-C. In 12-, 16-, 20-, 28-, and .410-gauges. Top-lever single-barrel visible hammer, automatic ejector. *By Savage Arms.*

Fox Model B. Hammerless double barrel in 12-, 16-, 20-, and .410-gauges. Ventilated rib. *By Savage Arms.*

Stevens 77-AC. In 12-, 16-, and 20-gauges, pump gun with adjustable choke and recoil pad. *By Savage Arms.*

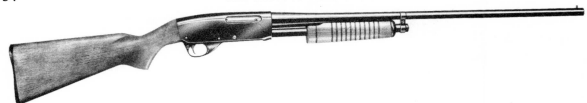

Stevens 77-.410. Twenty-six-inch barrel modified for full choke. *By Savage Arms.*

Stevens 77. In 12-, 16-, 20-, and .410-gauges. Pump gun chambered for 2¾- and three-inch shells in 12- and 20-gauges, 2¾-inch in 16-gauge, 2½- and three-inch in .410. *By Savage Arms.*

Stevens 59. .410 six-shot bolt action. *By Savage Arms.*

Stevens 58-AC. In 12-, 16-, and 20-gauges. Same as 58 but with adjustable choke. *By Savage Arms.*

Stevens 58-.410. Three-shot detachable clip magazine. Carries fourth shell in chamber. Weighs 5½ pounds. *By Savage Arms.*

Stevens 58 bolt action. In 12-, 16-, and 20-gauges. Chambered for 2¾-inch shells. Capacity three shells, including one in chamber. Weighs 7¼ pounds. *By Savage Arms*.

Stevens 51. .410 single-shot. Bolt action. Weighs 4¾ pounds. Automatic safety. *By Savage Arms*.

Savage 24-V combination rifle shotgun chambered for 20-gauge 2¾- and three-inch shells. Full choke in lower barrel. Upper barrel 222 Remington. Weighs 6¾ pounds. *By Savage Arms*.

Savage 24-S. 20-, .410 with rifle barrel for .22 long rifle or .22 Magnum. Side lever opening. *By Savage Arms*.

Savage 24-DL. Combination rifle shotgun chambering 20 or .410 shells in 2¾- or three-inch, and .22 long rifle upper barrel. Weighs 6¾ pounds. *By Savage Arms*.

Savage 30-T. Pump-action repeating 12-gauge trap gun with Montecarlo stock and recoil pad. Ventilated rib. Weighs eight pounds. *By Savage Arms.*

Savage 30-L. Pump-action 12-gauge for left-handed shooters. Chambers three-inch shells. Ventilated rib. In 12-, 20- and .410-gauges. *By Savage Arms.*

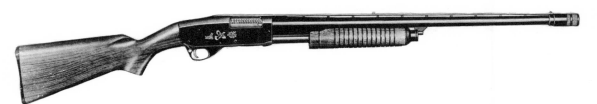

Savage 30-AC. Same as Savage Model 30 but with adjustable choke. *By Savage Arms.*

Savage 30-.410. *By Savage Arms.*

Savage 30. In 12-, 20-, and .410-gauges. Chambered for three-inch shells. Ventilated rib. *By Savage Arms.*

(Top) Franchi. Hunter grade autoloader. Ventilated rib. In 12-, 20-gauges. Chambered for 2¾-inch shells. Interchangeable barrel. Lightweight. Chrome-lined barrel. 20-gauge weighs five pounds, two ounces; 12-gauge weighs six pounds, four ounces. (Bottom) Franchi standard Aristocrat over-and-under. In 12-gauge. Barrels twenty-six, twenty-eight, or thirty inches. *By Stoeger Arms Corp.*

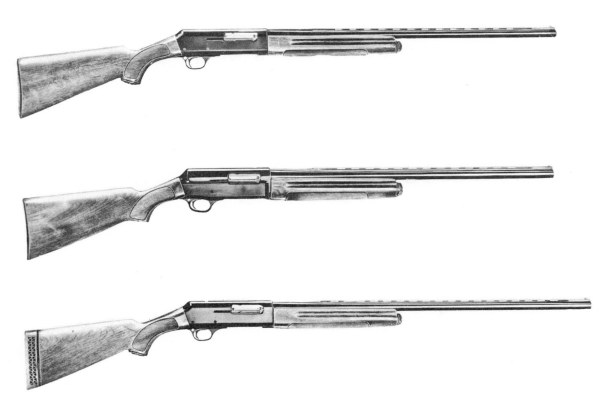

Franchi autoloaders. Top to bottom: 20-gauge standard model with ventilated rib; 12-gauge standard model with ventilated rib; 20-gauge Magnum. Interchangeable barrels. *By Stoeger Arms Corp.*

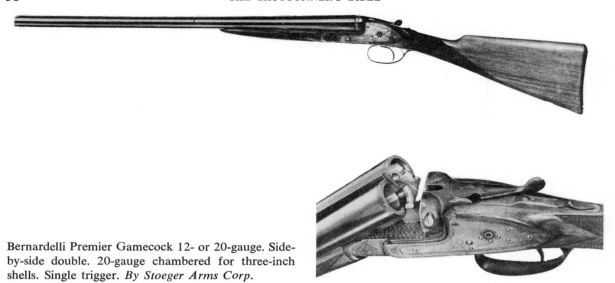

Bernardelli Premier Gamecock 12- or 20-gauge. Side-by-side double. 20-gauge chambered for three-inch shells. Single trigger. *By Stoeger Arms Corp.*

Franchi autoloaders. Top to bottom: 12-gauge Magnum; 12-gauge hunter with solid rib; 12-gauge Eldorado. Interchangeable barrels. *By Stoeger Arms Corp.*

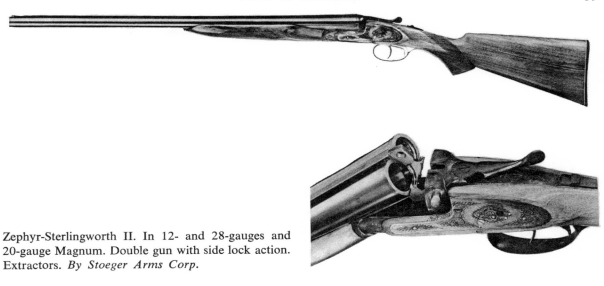

Zephyr-Sterlingworth II. In 12- and 28-gauges and 20-gauge Magnum. Double gun with side lock action. Extractors. *By Stoeger Arms Corp.*

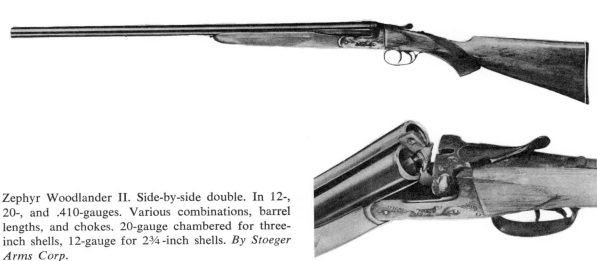

Zephyr Woodlander II. Side-by-side double. In 12-, 20-, and .410-gauges. Various combinations, barrel lengths, and chokes. 20-gauge chambered for three-inch shells, 12-gauge for 2¾-inch shells. *By Stoeger Arms Corp.*

Stoeger Model 27 trap gun. Thirty-two-inch barrel with ventilated rib. Montecarlo stock. Weighs 8¼ pounds. 12-gauge chambered for 2¾-inch shells. *By Stoeger Arms Corp.*

(Top) Stoeger Model 27 trap gun. (Bottom) Franchi trap model Aristocrat. Chrome-lined thirty-inch barrels. Weighs 8¼ pounds. *By Stoeger Arms Corp.*

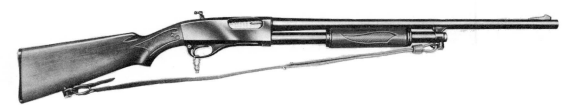

Noble 166L deer gun. Especially for use with rifled slugs. 12-gauge twenty-four-inch barrel suitable only for 2¾-inch Magnum shells. Capacity six shells. Slide action *By Noble Manufacturing Co.*

Model 66RCLP. In 12- and 16-gauges with twenty-eight-inch barrel. Ventilated rib. Chambered for three-inch Magnum 12-gauge, 2¾-inch Magnum 16-gauge. *By Noble Manufacturing Co.*

Noble Model 420. Side-by-side double. In 12-, 16-, and 20-gauges, with twenty-eight-inch barrels. Right barrel modified, left barrel full choke. 12-, 16-, 20-gauge with twenty-six-inch barrels, right barrel improved cylinder, left barrel modified. .410 with twenty-six-inch barrel only. *By Noble Manufacturing Co.*

Noble Model 602. 20-gauge with twenty-eight-inch barrel, ventilated rib. Slide action. Capacity six shots. Weighs 6½ pounds. *By Noble Manufacturing Co.*

Noble Model 70. .410-gauge slide action, twenty-six-inch barrel. Weighs six pounds. *By Noble Manufacturing Co.*

Noble Model 662. 20-gauge aluminum pump gun with twenty-eight-inch barrel. Chambered for 2¾-inch shells. Six-shot capacity. Weighs 4½ pounds. *By Noble Manufacturing Co.*

Winchester-Western Model 1200 field gun. Available in 12-, 16-, and 20-gauges. Slide action. *By Winchester-Western.*

Winchester 101 over-and-under field grade gun with ventilated rib. Single selective trigger. Selective ejection. In 12- and 20-gauge. *By Winchester-Western.*

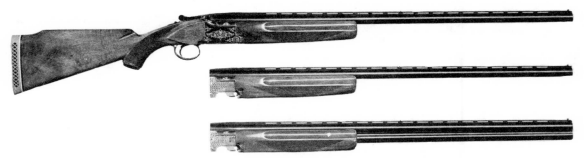

Winchester 101 over-and-under double. In 12- and 20-gauge. *By Winchester-Western.*

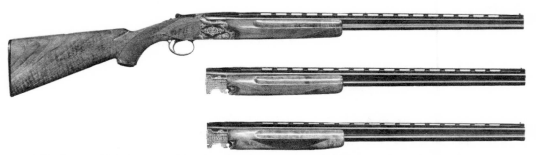

Winchester 101 skeet combination. In .410-, 28-, and 20-gauge. Interchangeable barrels. *By Winchester-Western.*

Winchester 21 super pigeon grade. Ventilated rib. Montecarlo stock. In 12-gauge only. Twenty-six-inch, twenty-eight-inch and thirty-inch barrels. *By Winchester-Western.*

Winchester Model 21 Grand American. In 12-, 16-, and 20-gauge. Double barrel. *By Winchester-Western.*

Winchester 1200 deer gun. In 12-gauge. Slide action. *By Winchester-Western.*

Winchester 1400 three-shot gas-operated autoloader. In 12-, 16-, and 20-gauges. *By Winchester-Western.*

Winchester 1200 three-inch Magnum. In 12- and 20-gauges. *By Winchester-Western.*

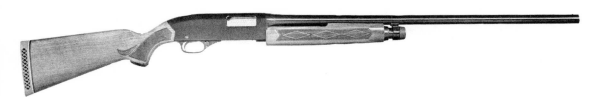

Winchester 1200 field grade with recoil reduction system. In 12-gauge. *By Winchester-Western.*

Winchester 1400 trap gun. In 12-gauge. Montecarlo stock with recoil reduction system. *By Winchester-Western.*

Remington 1100SA skeet gun. In 12-gauge. Five-shot. *By Remington Arms Co.*

Remington Model 1100 autoloading shotgun. In 12-gauge. Five-shot. *By Remington Arms Co.*

Remington Model 1100TB autoloading trap gun with ventilated rib. In 12-gauge. *By Remington Arms Co.*

Remington Model 1100 autoloading Magnum duck gun chambered for three-inch shells. In 12-gauge. Ventilated rib. *By Remington Arms Co.*

Remington Model 1100 deer gun. In 12-gauge. Autoloader. *By Remington Arms Co.*

Remington Model 870 Magnum duck gun. Pump action. Chambered for three-inch shells. In 12-gauge. *By Remington Arms Co.*

Remington Model 870TB pump action trap gun in 12-gauge with Montecarlo stock. *By Remington Arms Co.*

Remington Model 870 "Wingmaster" trap gun, five shot, in 12-gauge only. *By Remington Arms Co.*

Remington Model 870TB trap special grade, five shot, in 12-gauge only. *By Remington Arms Co.*

Remington "Brushmaster" Model 870 deer gun, in 12-gauge with twenty-inch rifle sight barrel. *By Remington Arms Co.*

Remington Model 870 "Wingmaster" pump action shotgun. In 12-gauge. Five-shot.
By Remington Arms Co.

Remington Model 1100 autoloading shotgun, small-bore version: 28- and .410-gauges.
By Remington Arms Co.

modern pump gun is equipped with a cylinder-type magazine in which shells rest end to end in a horizontal row beneath the barrel. The forearm slides backward and forward to eject the spent shell and run the next one into the chamber. With a little practice this becomes a smooth action easily accomplished without removing the gun from the shoulder.

Pump guns can be loaded with a single shell in the chamber plus up to five in the magazine. Federal waterfowl hunting regulations, it should be remembered, limit the hunter to a maximum of three shells in his gun at any one time, and plugs are available for limiting the magazines to this capacity.

AUTOLOADERS

The highly popular autoloader is a hard-working machine. A simple pull of the trigger not only fires the shell in the chamber, but also sets up a mechanism that flips it out of the gun, runs a fresh load into the chamber, and locks it ready for the next shot. Consequently, the shooter equipped with an autoloader can shoot as fast as he can pull the trigger. These guns are sometimes referred to as automatics, but they are not automatics. Automatics will fire shells one after the other as long as the shooter holds the trigger

down. The autoloading shotguns, therefore, are actually semiautomatic.

In recent years the semiautomatic has gained considerable popularity. There are a number of good reasons. They are moderately priced, somewhere between the range of pump guns and doubles. Being single-barrels, they can be equipped with any of the variable choke devices. For the average outdoorsman, the autoloader is the fastest shooting gun he can buy. It may be that he seldom needs the third shot. Perhaps he should use it fewer times than he does. But the fact remains that it is there, and another pull of the trigger puts it to work. It is often useful in waterfowl hunting. Autoloaders are highly popular with skeet shooters as well as hunters.

There are two types of mechanisms used in autoloading shotguns. The oldest one, which was utilized by Browning in making the first autoloader, brought out in 1905, ejects and reloads by harnessing the force of the recoil. This force activates a spring built into the stock. The series of jobs performed includes throwing out the empty, recocking the hammer, and running the next shell into the chamber. Owners of such guns who have occasional trouble with jamming should remember that the proper operation of this gun depends on holding it firmly against the shoulder. In the excitement of the moment it sometimes happens that the gun is not firmly shouldered, and consequently the reloading mechanism does not perform smoothly.

The other system utilized by autoloading shotguns is the gas-operated mechanism. For many years gun designers felt they should be able to bleed off a portion of the pressure created by the burning powder to operate the gun's action. This was first accomplished with military rifles and later adapted to shotguns. Recent models especially are noted for their soft recoil.

The gas used in this system is allowed to escape through a small hole in the bottom of the barrel into a cylinder ahead of the chamber where it compresses a piston. This sets up a series of actions that end with the new shell in the chamber ready for the next shot. Gas used to activate the reloading mechanism does not take any power away from the load of shot. This type of autoloader seldom gives trouble with jamming, but if it does the fault may be either with a clogged-up gas port, dirt in the action, or a broken ejector, which a good gunsmith can usually correct in a matter of minutes. There is every indication that this style of shotgun action will continue to gain favor.

Chapter 3

GAUGE

The gauge of a shotgun indicates the inside diameter of its bore. There are five commonly designated shotgun bores, the 10-, 12-, 16-, 20-, 28-gauge, and the .410. The .410 is not designated as the others, but instead refers to the caliber in inches, as a rifle's size is designated.

Gauge is an old-fashioned method of designating bore size, and indicates the number of lead balls of the diameter of the barrel needed to weigh one pound. A lead ball capable of fitting into the barrel of a 12-gauge shotgun should weigh one-twelfth of a pound. Designating the .410 in gauge would get a little clumsy because the pound of lead would work out to 67½ balls of the appropriate diameter.

There was a time when larger-gauge shotguns were in use than those found today in the fields and on the range. When waterfowl were still hunted for the market, the 10-gauge was a favorite among duck hunters. But its muzzle blast and recoil were considerable, and the weight of the gun was such that it was not easily handled by the average shooter. Modern three-inch magnums for the 12-gauge make it capable of whatever the field grade 10-gauge once performed, although those who still shoot the 10-gauge can obtain magnum loads for these guns as well. The 10-gauge should be on the official endangered species list. There is little chance it will ever stage a comeback because ammunition has become increasingly effective, and the trend in guns has been toward lighter weights and small gauges.

12-Gauge

For a large majority of American shotgun owners the 12-gauge is *the* gun. Somewhat heavier than the 16-gauge, it is still light enough for the average man to carry all day in the field. And with the variety of shells available, the 12 becomes a versatile implement, especially when equipped with a variable choke device. In short,

the one-gun man, unless quite small physically, will probably not do better than a 12-gauge choice providing he intends to hunt a wide variety of game and perhaps engage in target shooting as well.

If he will not practice much waterfowl or wild turkey hunting, and will concentrate instead on

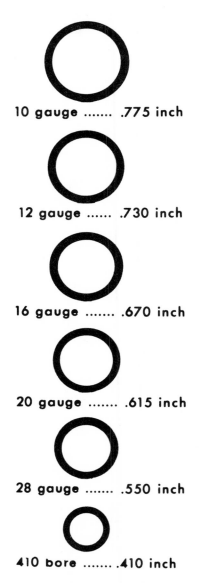

10 gauge .... .775 inch

12 gauge ...... .730 inch

16 gauge .... .670 inch

20 gauge .... .615 inch

28 gauge .... .550 inch

410 bore .... .410 inch

This chart shows the comparative diameters of shotgun barrels of various cases. (Actual size.) Converting gauge to measurement in inches. *By Winchester-Western.*

quail and other upland game, a 16- or 20-gauge may be entirely satisfactory for his field gun. Trap shooting is done with a 12-gauge.

For many hunters the 16-gauge is an excellent compromise between the 12 and the smaller shotguns. It will do about as much as the 12-gauge, is somewhat lighter and consequently easier to carry and handle, and it fires with less apparent recoil. Every so often someone ventures the opinion that the 16 is on the way out, but one sees so many of these guns in the hunting fields that it is hard to believe they are disappearing.

The 16-gauge magnum shell carrying 1¼ ounces of shot in the 2¾-inch length becomes an effective gun for taking waterfowl over decoys. And bored full choke it can be suitable for pass shooting as well, although here a 12-gauge is a better choice.

This gauge is frequently used on deer in the southeastern states with buckshot. In the heavy brush, shots usually come at close range, often twenty yards or closer, as the whitetail breaks through the palmettos ahead of hounds or the drivers. It is also an effective deer gun when loaded with rifled slugs. To my thinking, however, any smaller gauge is a questionable choice for taking deer with slugs.

Hunters in the more open areas of the country, where birds often rise fifty yards or so ahead of the gun, frequently prefer the 12-gauge over the 16 because of its added reach.

As for the 28-gauge, this gun is somewhere in between and has never become highly popular. One of my hunting companions recently expressed the opinion that "The 28-gauge is half too little and half not big enough." It is possible, however, to obtain 28-gauge loads which carry an ounce of shot in a 2¾-inch shell, and such loads do

Most popular and most versatile of the gauges is the 12, such as this waterfowl hunter carries. *By George Laycock.*

make the 28-gauge a suitable upland game gun in skilled hands. It is a pleasure to carry in the field. It is also used by some skeet shooters.

The .410-caliber feels like a toy gun after you handle a 12-gauge. Its suitability for field use is limited. Game effectively hunted with the .410 is limited mostly to small species easily killed at close range.

Some years ago half a dozen of us assembled on a newly opened shooting preserve to try the flighted mallard shooting. One of the older shooters arrived with his trusty little .410, which is not considered a waterfowling piece in most circles. The fact that he scored somewhat better than some of the rest of us with our larger gauges did nothing to convert me to the .410 for duck shooting. Nor would I advise anyone else to try the .410 on larger game of this kind. It was not created for the task.

Ammunition commonly available for use in the .410 includes both the 2½-inch shell carrying one-half ounce of shot, and the three-inch shell with three-quarter ounces of shot. The diameter of the pattern thrown by these loads is the same as the patterns made by larger gauges with similar degrees of choke, but obviously the density of the patterns will be lighter because the shells carry fewer pellets to spread over the same pattern area. This, in turn, means less chance of a clean kill or break with the smaller guns.

Frequently this is the gauge suggested as a beginner's gun for a boy or girl. About the only thing to recommend it for this purpose is its light weight and ease of handling. Scoring consistently with a .410 calls for the abilities of an expert. It is coming into increasing prominence on the skeet range only because it is the advanced shooter's gun. For anything else, a far better choice for those wanting a lightweight shotgun for general use might be a 20-gauge.

Chapter 4

SIGHTS

Over the years there has been an amazing collection of shotgun sights brought to the market. Most of these did not prove to have significant value. But the subject of shotgun sights should not be lightly dismissed, because some of them can be helpful.

The most common sighting aid on shotguns is the simple bead in any of various colors, customarily mounted on the barrel or rib near the gun's muzzle. The actual value of the bead, plus a second one sometimes lined up with it farther back on the barrel, is often questioned. Shooters argue about whether they see or do not see the beads, consciously or subconsciously. There are various improvements on the design of the bead, including replacements made of light-colored blocks of plastic designed to be more easily seen than the metal bead.

Many shooters insist on a rib on the top of the shotgun barrel or, in the case of double-barrels, between the barrels. The rib, a narrow strip of metal, provides a plane along which to sight. Mounted on little metal supports, it is kept out of direct contact with the barrel, and cooling air can pass beneath it. Remington field representative Ken Berger, a noted marksman on the trap ranges as well as a hunter, once compared the

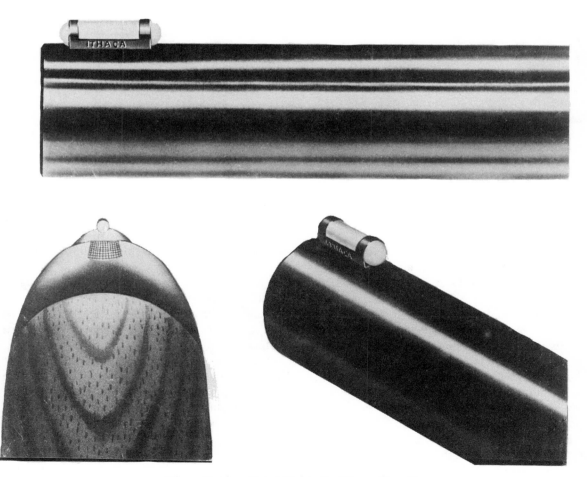

Ithaca Raybar Front Sight. *By Ithaca Gun Co.*

Deer hunter with scope mounted on shotgun. Remington 879 12-gauge pump gun. *By George Laycock.*

ventilated rib on his shotgun to a railroad track. "Your eye," he said, "follows right down the rails and stays lined up."

Some years ago Bill Weaver of W. R. Weaver Co., El Paso, Texas, created and marketed a scope sight which has been highly accepted by shotgunners. Weaver's K1 does not magnify the images. The initial reaction to such a device might be to question the value of a scope sight that does not magnify. For the shotgunner, it can do a lot of good things.

The K1 looks much like any other scope sight. Looking into the tube, the shooter sees two heavy crosshairs with a dot in the center. When the dot is on target, the gun is lined up. By following the course of the dot with his eye, the shooter can also use it as a point of reference in judging lead on moving targets. Although only one eye sees through the sight, both eyes can be, and should

be, open. Even if the shooter fails to cheek his gunstock at the same identical spot each time, the scope corrects the mistake because the aim is accurate as long as the eye sees into the scope. The scope has a ninety-six-foot field of vision at one hundred yards, and the ocular is adjustable to the shooter's eye.

Such a sight is especially good when shooting slugs in deer hunting, but is also valuable in bird hunting.

One of the newest sighting aids to appear is the Bi-Ocular Sight. In spite of its small size, the Bi-Ocular Sight is impressive because it is optically sound and it works. Made to replace the front bead on a shotgun barrel, it is a small glass lens about half an inch long resting in a metal cradle. It is especially useful in overcoming cross-shooting with both eyes open, because only the sighting eye sees the colored spot.

Model 1200 Winchester equipped with Williams Receiver Sight giving choice of open sight blade or peep. *By Williams Gun Sight Co.*

K1 Weaver-Scope mounted on gun. *By W. R. Weaver Co.*

Weaver-Scope Model K1, length 9½ inches. *By W. R. Weaver Co.*

Chapter 5

BARRELS

Modern shotgun barrels are manufactured to critical specifications from fluid steel of high quality, under rigidly controlled conditions. Some of the older gun barrels, and there are some still around, do not measure up in strength or safety features to these modern tubes. Occasionally an old-time Damascus shotgun barrel, intended for use with black powder, is given a test firing by some admiring and inquisitive descendant of the original owner who happens across the family heirloom in the attic of the old homestead. Said descendant just may get cut, bruised, burned, or frightened silly because such antiques under the pressure of modern ammunition can burst wide open.

Some of the early Damascus gun barrels were beautiful examples of metalwork. They were formed by welding alternate thin bands of steel and iron together, then forging and fusing them around a rod which determined the size of the bore. The resulting barrels were worked down and polished. But they usually had built-in weaknesses because controls over the quality of metals were primitive by modern standards, and under a magnifying glass the pits and corrosion in them are often easily visible.

But the Damascus barrels were still quite suitable for the work expected of them with black powder. Shells of the day, loaded with black powder, developed breech pressures of about six thousand pounds per square inch. Modern smokeless powder may build up pressures twice that high, with minimum pressures at least 50 percent higher than the black powders developed. In addition, the old Damascus guns usually had chambers too short for today's standard 2¾-inch shells. These conditions should make it evident that loading such an antique firearm with modern ammunition is folly.

The owner of such a gun should permit it to rest at peace in retirement. To make certain one of his friends or descendants does not test it at some future date, he should remove the firing pin or otherwise render it inoperative.

The modern shotgun barrels offered across the counters commonly come in three sizes—twenty-six, twenty-eight, or thirty inches. Some are thirty-two inches. There was a time when shotgunners believed that the length of the gun barrel had something to do with the wallop the gun would deliver; longer-barreled guns were said to be the hardest shooters. Careful ballistics tests have disproved this.

Engineers assure us that when a modern load is fired in a standard shotgun it builds up maximum pressure considerably short of the muzzle. This is usually accomplished in the first twenty inches of the barrel or less. Once the shot charge reaches maximum speed there is nothing a longer barrel might do to add more speed.

For this reason the choice of barrel length should rest on some other, and more legitimate factors. A longer barrel moves the muzzle blast farther from the shooter's ears. It also provides a somewhat better sighting plane for the long shots. On the other hand, a shorter barrel is more easily handled in thick cover.

But there is still the matter of balance. The gun should feel right in the hands, and a barrel that is especially long may be slow to handle. In addition, the gun with a barrel too short or light may not swing smoothly. For these reasons manufacturers seldom deviate far from accepted standard barrel lengths. In general, the longer gun barrels are chosen by those who wield 12-gauge shotguns on waterfowl or other targets that may call for an occasional long shot. The shorter barrels are usually found on guns used for upland game or bird hunting where fast gun handling is essential to effective shooting.

The shotgun owner who is a one-gun man will usually be better satisfied all around with a shorter barrel, preferably the twenty-six-inch length.

Gun owners should remember that the steel used in shotgun barrels is subject to denting and bending rather easily. It is a relatively soft steel and should not be abused.

Choke

Choke in a shotgun is the boring of the tube so the muzzle end is of a smaller diameter than the rest of the barrel. Perhaps no one will ever know for certain what pioneering shooter first decided that he could get a tighter pattern and reach out with longer shots by restricting the diameter of the muzzle. It is frequently said that the man was Fred Kimble, who was a duck hunter of almost legendary abilities.

But if Kimble were around to talk on the subject, the chances are he would set the record straight and admit that he was not the first to utilize the idea of choke. Joseph W. Long of Boston, a shooting companion of Kimble, claimed that back in 1827, a gunsmith named Jeremiah Smith discovered the merits of choke in Smithfield, Rhode Island.

Kimble and Long went hunting together in 1867 when Kimble carried an 11-gauge muzzle-loader that weighed nine pounds and had a bored cylinder. He did creditably with it on ducks at moderate range but poorly on the long shots.

Before Long departed for Boston both hunters decided to have new guns made before the next year, and each gun was to be bored to shoot "as close as possible."

Each man would test his gun with four drams of powder and one ounce of No. 4 shot fired at a target one foot square at forty yards. Fred Kimble went out with several of his friends who carried along their own guns, and he outshot them all badly. In Boston, Long also was happy with the tight pattern of his new gun.

Kimble's fame began to spread among shooters. It was in the spring of 1872 that he and Long joined five other friends in the flooded grain fields along the Sangamon River. Kimble carried his new 9-gauge single-shot with its special choke boring. In seventeen days the group brought down 2760 ducks. Of these, Kimble shot 1365.

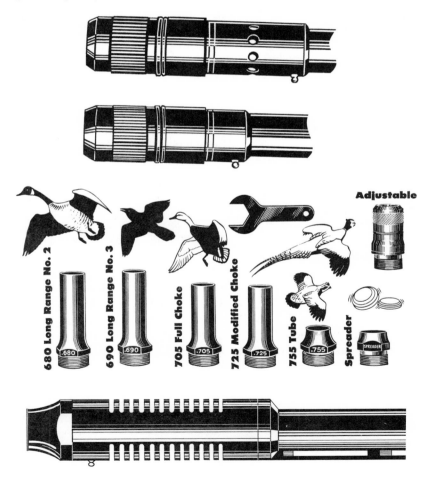

Lyman Choke Adapters (top and center) and Cutts Compensator (bottom). *By Lyman Gun Sight Corp.*

The word spread. Kimble passed the secret along to a gunsmith friend, L. J. Johnson, who advertised his services adjusting shotguns to shoot tighter patterns.

When word of this first filtered to the Midwest gunsmiths, they laughed about it. Meanwhile, Johnson was working long hours. Eventually other gunsmiths began boring gun barrels for choke too.

Regardless of who first built choke into gun barrels, the idea in its present form permits shooters to choose a degree of choke best matched to their needs. The four commonly designated choke borings in shotguns today are cylinder, improved cylinder, modified, and full choke.

It should be noted, however, that choke alone does not determine how a gun shoots. The ammunition plays a major role, and in recent years new developments in the building of superior shotshells improved the patterns shooters were able to get with their guns. Prior to choke boring, patterns of 35–40 percent were about as good as you could expect, but today a shooter can possibly obtain 85 percent patterns, which are probably too tight for most of his shots.

The choke in a gun barrel is confined to the first four inches or less of the muzzle. It is not a constriction visible to the human eye or revealed by the probing finger, and there's no substance to the old idea that a dime can be used to measure a full choke. The standard bore of a 12-gauge shotgun is .729 inch, and a constriction of about .035 inch will convert it to a full-choke barrel. Actually, from one manufacturer to the next, both the cylinder diameter and the choke boring may vary, and the relationship between them is more significant than the actual measurements.

Patterns

The casual shotgun owner who may shoot only a few times a year seldom gives a second thought to what the group of pellets coming from his gun may look like under varying conditions. But the fact remains that by giving a little attention to the shooting characteristics of his gun he might improve his marksmanship because he would understand his gun better. The first thing a really experienced shotgun purchaser does with a new gun is take it out for a few hours of test shooting in which his primary aim is to determine what kind of patterns it throws.

Not all guns of the same degree of choke throw identical patterns. There are, in fact, some astounding differences found between guns which, judging by the choke designation stamped on the barrel, should shoot alike. Different manufacturers turn out gun barrels bored to different diameters within the same gauge and choke specification. In two 12-gauge barrels both bored "full choke" there may be as much as .030-inch variation, or more.

Other variables that can further affect the pattern include the design of the choke boring, and the type loads being shot. Consequently, it is little wonder that a session of patterning a shotgun often turns up surprises.

Shotguns are normally patterned at forty yards, but the fact is that this is an extreme range for many kinds of upland shooting. Some shooters, even those who may have outfitted themselves with full-choke guns, seldom take shots more than thirty yards distant, and many of his shots are likely to be closer to twenty yards. For this practical reason it is a good idea, in addition to patterning the gun at the standard forty-yard distance, to do some additional test shooting with various loads of your choice at ten, fifteen, and twenty yards. This is when you begin to understand how small the pattern may actually be on those close-up shots, and consequently how accurate your shooting has to be, especially if your gun is bored full choke or even modified.

What shooters sometimes fail to recognize is that a load of shot heading for a target does not describe a flat, disk-shaped pattern. This is the impression gained from shooting into a sheet of paper, but in fact some of the shot reaches the mark considerably ahead of the rest of it. The shot strings out as it travels. Depending on the range, the load, and the choke, the shotstring may extend along the path for several feet. This is one reason accounting for the fact that leading a flying target too far is less often a cause of misses than is shooting behind the target. The target or bird may fly into the end of the string of shot. A short shotstring concentrates the pellets and means either more clean kills or clean misses, either of which is more desirable than a cripple.

The choke of a gun barrel is usually expressed in shot percentages that fall within a thirty-inch circle at forty yards.

65%–75%	Full choke
55%–65%	Modified
45%–55%	Improved cylinder
35%–45%	Cylinder bore

Finding the range where your shotgun belongs in this scale is fairly simple. Obtain a large board to which you can attach large sheets of paper. Set up the patterning board and measure off a forty-yard shooting distance. Determine in advance the kinds of loads you want to test, and keep records of each one as you test-fire them and check the patterns.

After firing a shot into a clean sheet of paper, determine where the greatest concentration of pellets struck. From this point inscribe a circle thirty inches in diameter. Then count the number of pellets falling within the circle. Compare this figure with the number of pellets in the load. From this compute the percentage of the total pellets within the circle.

This session of patterning could be the most important time you spend in getting set for the upcoming hunting seasons.

Shooters, especially those with limited experience, frequently buy full-choke guns when they should buy some other type of barrel. Their reason is generally that full choke will enable them to make clean kills on longer shots. The shotgun, however, is essentially a short-distance gun, and many shooters make their kills or break their targets at shorter distances than they like to believe. The choice of a choke should depend on the kind of game or targets, and the average distances at which you hope to score. If you will do only pass shooting at high-flying waterfowl, the full choke may indeed be the gun for you. If, on the other hand, you want a general-purpose gun, a full-choke tube definitely is not the right choice. The pattern may be entirely too tight for the fifteen- or twenty-yard shot at a pheasant or rabbit, and result either in a clean miss or in an animal blasted into a useless condition. For the average shotgunner, choosing a single-barrel shotgun for general-purpose shooting, it is hard to beat a modified choke.

There are a couple of ways, however, to have a wider choice of barrels on the same gun. One is to buy a gun with interchangeable barrels so the tubes can be switched depending on the type of shooting scheduled for the day. With this kind of gun you can go from full choke for pass shooting to modified for upland game with a minimum of time or trouble.

Another plan is to purchase a double-barrel with the barrels bored for different chokes. The first barrel can fire a pattern that opens up sooner, and the second one a tighter pattern effective at somewhat greater ranges.

For the average shotgunner who uses the same gun for a wide variety of shooting, a variable choke selector is a common solution to the problem. One choice is the Poly-Choke which a gunsmith, or the factory, can install on the end of any single barrel of 12-, 16-, or 20-gauge. It can be turned to select the desired degree of constriction in the muzzle. Another system is employed by the Cutts Compensator, which is a set of tubes of different diameter boring. A shooter can change tubes depending on the kind of shooting he faces. With either type choke adjustor the gun becomes more versatile than it could otherwise be.

Gun owners who want their shotgun barrels bored to shoot tighter patterns, for example to change it from improved cylinder to modified, can have it jug bored by a gunsmith.

It is always a good idea to pattern a newly acquired choke device to see that it is throwing patterns designated at its various settings.

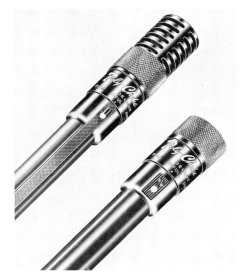

(Top) Deluxe ventilated Poly-Choke with recoil reducing sleeve. In 12-, 16-, and 20-gauges. Provides nine choke settings. (Bottom) Standard Poly-Choke, same as deluxe model but with no ventilated sleeve. *By Poly-Choke Co.*

Chapter 6

STOCKS

Good shotgun stocks are made almost exclusively of walnut, most of it from black walnut grown in the fertile soils of the central states. There is considerable danger that we are running short of walnut. A good walnut log measuring eight feet long and fifteen inches in diameter at breast height or higher brings one hundred dollars or more and may go into the manufacture of paneling or furniture as well as for gunstocks. The tree may at this point be between sixty and eighty years old. There is now tree breeding research under way to speed up the growth of black walnut so a good log can be produced in forty to forty-five years.

Walnut is not the only wood that can be made into gunstocks. Substitutes tried by gun manufacturers have included such woods as bird's-eye maple. Some manufacturers have built gunstocks

Block of walnut, which is favorite wood for gunstocks. *By American Walnut Manufacturers Association.*

with synthetic plastics. But in the eyes of many gun owners no satisfactory walnut substitute has ever been found.

Early guns, both fowling pieces and rifles, all had straight grips, but today shotgun stocks generally come with various degrees of pistol grip, one-fourth, one-half, or full. Pistol grips came into vogue abut 1850. Some hunters still prefer the straight-gripped gun for those long days in the field because such stocks make the gun more comfortable to carry. Such stocks also allow for quick adjustment when wearing gloves or for accommodating hands that are especially large or small.

Skeet and trap shooters, who generally have their guns in shooting position or nearly so before the target is called, find the half or full pistol grip suitable. The pistol grip does permit holding the gun in a more positive natural position. The one-quarter grip is a good all-around design.

How does a shotgun purchaser go about determining the best stock measurements for his use? Some English gun shops, plus a few in the United States, still employ "try" stocks. These are complicated measuring devices which a gunsmith adjusts to learn the desired measurements for building a custom-fashioned stock to the individual's order. But unless a gun buyer has a lot of money to spend on a shotgun he seldom considers having a stock fitted to order. The truth is that the manufacturers, after turning out millions of guns for millions of shooters, have arrived at standard stock measurements. Shooters pick and choose from the factory standard gunstocks until they find one that seems the best of the lot for them because it "feels" right. Although not a scientific procedure by most standards, this works amazingly well.

After obtaining a new gun, some shooters begin to shave and whittle at the comb of the stock until it conforms precisely to what they prefer. Trap shooters, who often shoot for money, constantly search for ways to improve the fit of their guns. No matter how much a person shoots, however, there are some fairly simple steps for getting a good fit with a shotgun.

Many shotgun stocks are manufactured to standard measurements of 14 by 2½ by 1⅝ inches. The fourteen-inch length of pull, which is the distance from trigger to butt plate, may call for some adjustment depending on the size of the shooter and the use to which he puts the gun. If

Ohio gunsmith, Charles Grossman, inspecting refinished gunstock. *By George Laycock.*

the shotgun stock is too long, it may hang up on a hunter's field clothing as he shoulders his gun, and if it is too short it can position the thumb on the grip so close to the face that his nose ends up helping absorb the recoil.

There are factory standard trap guns offered with stocks somewhat longer than the standard field-gun measurements. The trap shooter has the gun up and ready when he calls for the target so he knows he's not going to get tangled up in his shooting jacket. Dimensions common on trap-gun stocks are 14⅜ by 1½ inches at the comb and 1⅞ inches drop at the heel. There are also stocks available with slightly shorter lengths than the standard fourteen inches for the hunter who has to bundle up in heavy clothing. The standard measurement calls for a drop of 1⅝ inches at the comb and 2½ inches at the heel. The more important of these dimensions, so far as accurate shooting is concerned, is the measurement of the comb. Because the cheek is held against the comb, the comb's height determines the plane along which the shooter's master eye sights. Either too high or too low can result in pointing troubles.

The butt of the stock is cut at an angle that helps fit it to the shoulder. To get a better visual impression of what this does to the lines of the gun, try resting it on its butt plate on the floor

and moving it back until the breech touches the wall. The barrel will normally lean away from the wall at an angle. The pitch is the distance measured from the gun's muzzle to the wall. A normal pitch on a twenty-six-inch barrel is about 2 inches. Interestingly enough, this may vary in standard models from manufacturer to manufacturer, and sometimes even from the same production line. In actual practice this is seldom important to the average shooter unless he begins to install a recoil pad and wants to know at what angle he should cut the stock off.

Shooters who are either shorter, taller, or otherwise at variance with more or less typical adult male proportions, may need to make some adjustments in the measurements of the gunstocks. Such adjustments are made in fractions of an inch and they should preferably be administered by someone skilled in working with guns and shooters. It sometimes happens that a shotgun owner becomes dissatisfied with the fit of his gun although he may be unable to fathom the reason much less correct the fault. Charlie Grossman, a longtime professional gunsmith at Milford, Ohio, often gets visits from shooters seeking answers to such problems. "First," says Charlie, "I study the way the person holds a gun. Sometimes I have to watch him shoot. The elevation of the comb is the most important thing about the fit of the stock. On a rifle a shooter can work around until he gets the two sights lined up. But on a shotgun there's only one sight, the front bead or muzzle of the gun. The rear sight is the eye, and if it is in the wrong place the shooter is not going to score the way he wants to. The comb can hold the eye too high or too low.

"But there are a lot of things," Charlie added, "that figure into good shooting. Even the best shooters sometimes develop little traits that throw them off, and sometimes they can't figure out what it is by themselves. It may not be that they need changes in their guns at all. It may just be that by having somebody who is a good shot watch them they can discover what they're doing wrong.

"A person with a barrel chest or a big short neck," he says, "may need changes in the gun to make it fit him. If he has broader than normal cheekbones this may require adjustment in the stock."

Gunstocks, over the years, have undergone evolutionary changes, and perhaps the most surprising thing about those on the market today is that manufacturers have come up with mass-produced designs and measurements which, just as they come from the factory, are acceptable to the majority of shooters.

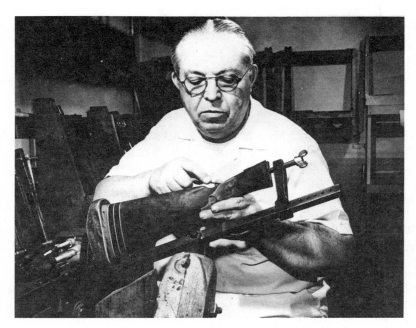

Checkering on expensive shotguns is done by hand, as this Ithaca craftsman demonstrates. Less expensive checkering is pressed into gunstock. *By Ithaca Gun Co.*

Chapter 7

RECOIL

A Missouri mule may kick for no reason at all, but the shotgun has an excuse. There is a well-known law of physics—Newton's Law—advising us that for every action there is a compensating reaction. The backward force of a shotgun against the shoulder of the shooter results from the forward motion of the shot propelled by the expanding powder gases.

The shape of the gun may affect the impact the shooter feels. Ballistics experts explain that the straighter the gunstock, the less the apparent recoil. This is due to the fact that a stock with considerable drop at the heel is forced up, as well as back, by the discharge.

If a change in ammunition does not correct the unpleasant apparent recoil, the owner can try equipping the gun butt with a recoil pad to serve as a shock absorber. Tournament shooters who fire many rounds of ammunition in a typical day customarily want their guns equipped with pads. For the field shooter who shoots far less in an average day's hunting, the recoil pad may be less necessary even if he uses magnum loads. But this is a matter of choice and something for the gun owner to determine for himself.

The recoil pad is generally installed by a gunsmith because part of the gunstock is removed to compensate for the thickness of the pad. The gun owner handy enough with hand tools can do the job himself.

Manufacturers of recoil pads, such as Pachmayr, supply directions for gun owners who want to tackle the alteration. Depending on the width of the pad, a compensating amount of wood must be removed from the butt of the stock. Otherwise, the length of pull is altered. The pitch line must first be determined for the gun, then the cut from the butt of the stock made at a ninety-degree angle to the pitch line. After the pad is secured to the stock with screws and ground to conform to the contour of the stock, it is often necessary to refinish the portion of the butt marred during the installation.

Various systems of venting the gas off at the muzzle have aided in reducing apparent recoil.

Other devices have also been created to cut down the amount of recoil felt by the shooter, and perhaps the biggest step in this direction was taken recently when inventor Ralph O. Hoge of Hollywood perfected his Hydra-Coil. The idea was one that Hoge created while working out systems to absorb shock during the operation of movie cameras so they would operate more smoothly. He saw no reason why it wouldn't work equally well for the age-old problem of reducing the recoil impact. Winchester-Western was one of the gun companies interested in the invention from its early days, and that company recently introduced the idea as a feature built into two of its most popular 12-gauge guns.

This recoil reduction system uses a two-part hollow stock made of plastic so that when the gun is fired the front part of the stock with the pistol grip is forced backward into the comb section. A mechanism inside the stock absorbs recoil with heavy springs and hydraulic cylinders. Winchester tests prompt the manufacturer to

Pachmayr Magnum Recoil Pad. *By Pachmayr Gun Works, Inc.*

Ithaca anti-recoil pad. *By Ithaca Gun Co.*

claim a recoil reduction as much as 78 percent for the system, and rate the apparent recoil from 12-gauge guns so equipped at 50 percent less than that of a standard 20-gauge. In addition to absorbing some of the shock, the device spreads the rest of the force over a longer period of time. This spreading of the force, which is in reality only a few thousandths of a second, means an impact which is not as sharp against the shoulder.

The shooter who fires both factory loads and home-loaded ammunition should be alert for differences in the recoil from the two. If the hand loads are either lighter or heavier, compared with factory loads, there may be a situation that calls for correction. Light recoiling may mean that the shot are not traveling with the velocity needed to render killing impact with game. Too much recoil could mean that the shells are overloaded and charge data should be double-checked.

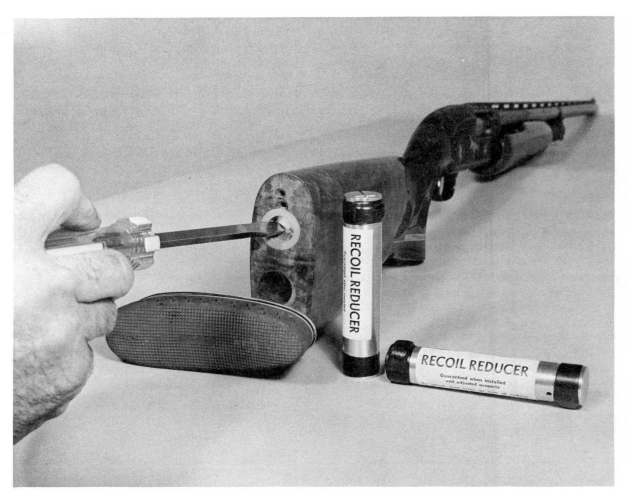

Edwards Recoil Reducer is installed in the stock of this gun. *By Edwards Recoil Reducer.*

Chapter 8

BUYING A SHOTGUN

Many a male citizen, short on patience when accompanying his wife on a shopping trip, is inclined to explain how shopping procedures should be streamlined. One way a wife can terminate such refrains, although we do not advise it, unless the purchase is for her, is to tag along when her husband buys a shotgun. This is the hour of truth. Each gun on the rack will be studied, hefted, fitted to the shoulder, and discussed. Providing the purchaser is serious about getting a new gun, this is as it should be. But he is better off to first do his homework and have an idea of which gun might best fit his needs. The shotgun is likely to be a long time in the family and go along on hunting trips and visits to target ranges for years to come.

First consider what you will use the gun for. It might range from squirrel hunting and trap shooting to hunting geese with heavy loads and perhaps deer with buckshot or slugs. Many outdoorsmen get along with a single shotgun in spite of a wide range of interests in the world of shooting.

This is where the basic question of gauge comes into the decision. Gauge, the measure of diameter of the barrel and consequently the ammunition, plays a major role in determining effective ranges and number of shot pellets in a load.

The gauges commonly offered are 10, 12, 16, 20, 28, and .410 caliber. In general, loaded with comparable standard factory ammunition, each step up in gauge size from the .410-caliber to the 10-gauge can be expected to add about five yards to the effective range of the gun. The rule of thumb says large gauges for large game, smaller ones for smaller game. But there are so many exceptions to this, because of ammunition, personal choices, and degrees of shooting skill that no one can safely say there is one best shotgun.

The average-sized man buying a gun for a wide variety of uses should probably settle on a 12-gauge. If he will not be doing much trap shooting, waterfowl or deer hunting, the 16- or 20-gauge might be better. The 20- or 28-gauge is often a good choice for upland game shooting, especially in brushy country where the shots are at relatively close range. The lighter guns are more easily handled, a bit faster in the hands of many shooters, and easier to carry for long periods.

The question of gun weight is related to the recoil the shooter will feel. A large-gauge gun especially light in weight may pound the shooter's shoulder unpleasantly. The more shooting he does the more he will notice it. Manufacturers, well aware of this, realize that the added weight is needed in guns shooting heavier loads. "We could," says one manufacturer, "make a four-

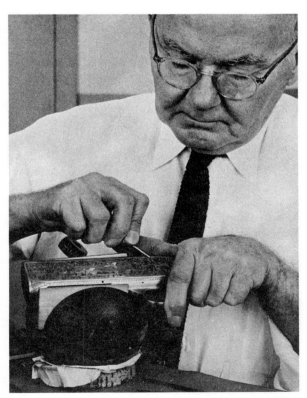

Prices on shotguns vary over a wide range. The highest-priced guns, such as this Ithaca three-thousand-dollar shotgun, receive long hours of handwork. Fortunately, except for the fancy work, the average shotgunner can own guns almost equal in quality. Shotguns have been meticulously tested all along the production line and usually have been given a final test-firing before shipment. *By Ithaca Gun Co.*

The sportsman setting out to buy a new shotgun has a wide range of choices in gauge, choke, weight, barrel length, and type of action. *By Winchester-Western.*

pound 16-gauge, but it would be unpleasant to shoot."

Barrel length may be less important than it is sometimes considered. Most shotgun barrels are twenty-six, twenty-eight, or thirty inches long. A long barrel does not ordinarily impart any added force to the shot propelled from the gun. In any event, the shot reaches its maximum velocity considerably short of the muzzle. What a couple of extra inches on the gun barrel might do for a shooter is provide him a better aiming plane along which to sight for those long pass shots. The twenty-eight-inch barrel is a good choice much of the time.

The standard shotgun chamber, except in the .410, is bored to accommodate 2¾- and three-inch shells. The gun purchaser who may want to use three-inch magnums, perhaps on waterfowl or wild turkeys, selects a gun chambered to receive the longer shells. He would never shoot these longer shells in guns chambered only for shorter ammunition.

One of the big questions in selecting a shotgun is to determine the amount of choke that should be built into the barrel. This restriction in the size of the barrel at the muzzle helps determine the pattern thrown by the gun at various distances. This subject is more fully discussed on page 57.

Some shotguns are designed with interchangeable barrels so shooters can make fast changes from one degree of choke to another where they may, for example, hunt both waterfowl and upland game on the same trip.

A good choice for the shooter who can own but one gun, is a single-barrel shotgun equipped with a selective choke device. The choke regulator is generally an extra that is installed by a gunsmith. Good gun stores often have their own gunsmiths who perform such jobs.

The shotgun purchaser also has a choice of actions. The well-stocked gun store will give him the opportunity to choose from single-barrel autoloaders, single-barrel bolt-action guns, single-barrel pump guns, and the doubles which will have the tubes either side-by-side or over-and-under.

Federal regulations limit the legal number of shells in a shotgun to three when hunting migratory waterfowl. Waterfowl hunters with guns capable of carrying more shells than this must plug them so they have to be disassembled to remove the plug.

As for the speed of getting off that second or third shot, a skilled pump gun shooter can be fast indeed. But the average gunner will find nothing faster than the autoloader. I have known grouse hunters who just assumed that for every grouse they kicked up they would spend three shells in rapid succession. They might never be happy with guns allowing them only one or two shots. But the added care needed in their shooting might bring an equal number of grouse to the pot.

It frequently happens that a potential shooter purchasing his first shotgun decides to settle for an inexpensive model in spite of the fact that it may not feel too good to him. His plans, once he learns to shoot better, to buy a better gun. He would be better off to get the better shotgun in the beginning if possible. He will shoot better, partly because he has more confidence in it.

This matter often comes into focus when a father buys a first gun for his boy, or a husband decides to equip his wife with a shotgun. These family members are to be introduced to the wonderful world of outdoor sports, the glories of an autumn day in the field, and the sense of personal accomplishment in accurate and effec-

tive shooting. A poorly fitted gun could discourage them at the very beginning.

A boy, girl, or woman will probably be less able to handle the weight of a 12-gauge than an adult male will. For upland shooting especially, the best choice for these beginners is often a good 20-gauge gun. Because these shooters may notice recoil more than the average experienced gunner, at least in their early efforts, the autoloaders, especially gas-operated models, should be considered. The mechanism tends to help absorb part of the recoil energy. To further soften recoil, the gun can be equipped with a good-quality shoulder pad, especially important if the gun will be used for target shooting, and consequently be shot a lot more than it might if limited to use in hunting.

It may well be, as some shooting coaches say, that proper shooting instruction is more important to the beginner than the choice of gun. But it does not follow that one must choose between

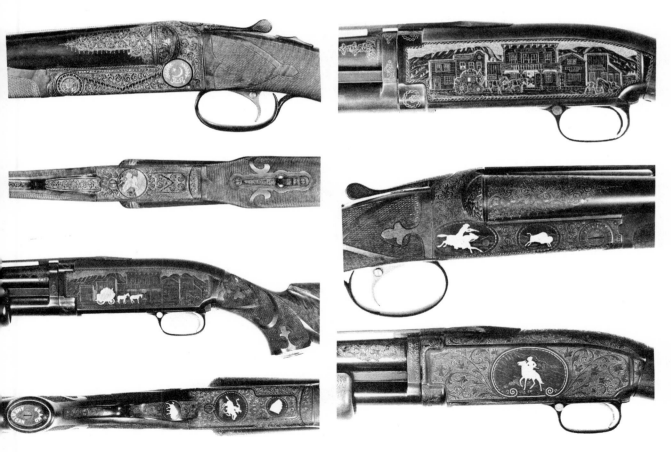

Some of the more famous detailed engravings that have been rendered on expensive Winchester-Western shotguns. *By Winchester-Western.*

the two. A well-fitted shotgun, coupled with friendly and skilled coaching and encouragement, puts the odds in the beginner's favor and strengthens chances that the new shooter will develop skill. If there is any serious question about fitting the shooter with standard factory stocks, the problem should be taken to a gunsmith who can fit the stock to the person.

There is, of course, one more factor in the selection of the gun, the price. The range of prices on shotguns, from the lowest-priced single-shots to the fancy hand-crafted skillfully engraved job, is understandably tremendous. It is possible, given the finances, to buy a shotgun for three thousand dollars or more. But for most of us it would probably shoot about the same as a standard gun off the sales rack. Modern manufacturing methods and mass production make it possible to buy a standard-grade autoloader for a price in the vicinity of $150. Pump guns are lower in price, with various models available in the $100 to $125 range, while a single-barrel, single-shot or bolt-action shotgun can be purchased for less than fifty dollars. Double-barrel guns are, generally speaking, among the highest-priced shotguns available, although there are some modestly priced doubles on the market, including the Fox double, which is priced competitively with the autoloaders and pump guns.

But the shotgun that goes home with you from the gun store may be in use thirty years later. Try dividing that thirty into the price of the best shotgun you can afford. You come out with a surprisingly low annual cost on a possession that can be the key to uncounted hours of shooting pleasure. Most of today's American-made, production-model shotguns are highly dependable. They are made by skilled workmen and the most modern machinery. They will do what the manufacturer claims. Before leaving the plant they are test-fired to see that they are functionally correct. The modern shotgun may undergo three thousand inspections during its construction, from examination of raw materials to final testing on the range. They are usually tested with ammunition 50 percent more powerful than standard factory loads. The manufacturer is as eager as the purchaser to have the gun perform smoothly over a long period of years.

You may not be able to afford the fancy engraving and other extras, but select a shotgun that fits right and will meet your needs on the range or in the field.

Chapter 9

SHOTGUN SHELLS

Those boxes of shotgun shells stacked on the shelves have a family history that goes back to a period shortly after the Civil War, when early efforts were under way to develop breech-loading shotguns. The muzzleloaders still lasted for a considerable time, partly because they were modest in price. At least one mail order house was still offering muzzleloaders—"in sizes for boys and men"—as late as 1900. The prices ranged from $2.50 each up to $8.00.

But the standard shotgun shell was already known and used everywhere. Some early shotshells were made of brass, and intended for the hand loader who could then pack the tube with whatever shot and powder he figured he needed for the job at hand. But it was not many years before shells evolved into a tube of tightly rolled paper inserted in a brass base or cup. Impregnating the paper with wax added moisture resistance and strength. This type of basic shotgun shell was not changed much until recent times, when designers began experimenting with plastic shells, new types of wads, and methods of crimping.

A cross section of the old standard-type shotgun shell not only shows the component parts needed but also gives some idea of the job each must do. The list of components includes the brass cup, primer, shell case, base wad, powder, shot, overpowder wad, filler wads and overshot wad. Some of these components have vanished from shells of recent design, while others have undergone radical changes since the introduction of such refinements as plastic shot sleeves.

Primers

The primer is a very small container of highly explosive chemical materials seated in the center of the shotshell base. How well it does its job plays a major role in the effectiveness of the shell, because the primer creates the heat needed to ignite the charge of powder. And the chemi-cals in the primer are ignited by the force of the firing pin as the trigger is pulled.

The main parts of the primer include a little cup to hold the chemicals, an anvil against which they are compressed under force of the firing pin, and a flash hole through which the hot gases escape to ignite the powder.

Inside the primer there is an entirely different type of chemical than there was some years ago. Once the mixture was made largely of potassium chlorate. This did the job, but it oxidized and created a salt by-product that stuck in the gun barrel where it attracted moisture. The result was rust in the gun barrel unless it was cleaned incessantly. Mercuric compounds which were later used also had serious drawbacks and were eventually replaced.

The modern priming mixture does all the things asked of it and does them well. Modern primers fire consistently and do their job so well that they are seldom given much thought by the average shotgun owner. He doesn't have to worry about them.

Obviously, the manufacture of priming mixtures can be a touchy process. The chemicals must be mixed and blended. The quantities must be large enough so that when thoroughly mixed the materials give absolutely uniform performance. And they must be capable of being handled without igniting before they are expected

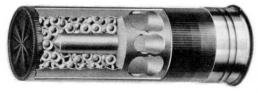

Remington special post wad for trap shooters to spread pattern for sixteen-yard shots. *By Remington Arms Co.*

Cutaway of high-base Remington shell. *By Remington Arms Co.*

Remington target load shown in cutaway drawing to reveal location of primer powder, plastic wad, and shot. *By Remington Arms Co.*

to. This is accomplished by mixing the chemicals with water. Working with them wet reduces the hazard. They can then be dried as one of the final steps in the process. The same chemicals are used in primers for rifle and handgun ammunition.

Gunpowder

The origin of gunpowder is lost, perhaps for all time, in the musty annals of man's past. There are records of it back to 1313. Saltpeter was an early component of these explosives, and our ancestors went to considerable trouble to obtain these materials. Some European peasants several centuries ago were required to pay part of their taxes in saltpeter, which it was learned could be produced by piling up organic materials like a compost heap and from time to time wetting them down, preferably with urine.

Black powder got its name from its charcoal content. But powder was a physical form not highly suited to good combustion properties, so in due time those ancients learned to granulate the powder. The granules burned better. Then with the advent of plastic materials the whole picture changed—for the better. The age of smokeless powder (the powder is neither powder nor smokeless) ushered in better materials for the shooter. Smokeless powder is created by mixing together nitric acid, sulphuric acid, and cellulose materials, all meticulously compounded, dried, blended, and finally tested.

The powders must burn with uniformity and with accelerating speed as pressure builds up in the gun chamber and barrel.

Smokeless powder can be stored indefinitely without deterioration provided it is kept in a cool and dry place. It should, of course, not be near open flame or stored where children might get into it.

How Shot Is Made

Those pellets of lead in shotshells are manufactured today in the same fashion they were made a half century and more ago. Old shot towers are still in use, and while material-handling methods have improved the efficiency of a few of the manufacturer's steps, the lead still goes through the same old steps from pig to pellet. Recently I rode the elevator to the top of Remington's unique twin shot tower to follow this procedure step by step. Les Hollos, who has supervised shot production in this tower for a quarter century, shouted above the rumbling of the machinery that, "Ninety percent of the equipment used here is the original equipment installed in 1909."

Les assured me that this is the only "twin" shot tower in business. Shot is dropped here from two identical towers twenty-four hours a day at the rate of twenty thousand pounds per hour in each tower. The bars of lead are fed to the top of the tower on a conveyor. Along with them go measured quantities of antimony and arsenic. The antimony for hardening, the arsenic for roundness.

The amount of antimony added to the lead determines the hardness of the shot. Two words frequently heard to describe hardness are "chilled" and "dropped." These are not very descriptive names. Chilled shot actually means shot containing 1 percent or more of antimony. Dropped shot, which is softer, contains less than 1 percent of antimony. Antimony is costly and, consequently, making shot harder adds to the cost of shotgun ammunition. More costly yet is the shot that is electroplated with copper. The bars of lead melt in a heated vat and the liquid feeds off steadily into pans that resemble iron skillets. They measure 1½ feet across, and the bottom of each shot pan is drilled full of holes. Some pans have large holes to produce the larger shot; others are drilled with small holes for forming fine shot.

Liquid lead forms in little beads on the bottom of the holes, then drops off. The lead shot falls down steadily like a heavy rain. The drop of 135 feet does nothing to shape the pellet but serves only to cool it. The shot falls into a tank of water at the bottom.

The purpose of the water is to cushion the shot so it will not lose its roundness. Then a conveyor gathers it up and transports it back to the third-story level so that it can flow by gravity through the remainder of the processing steps.

Graphite is added as a lubricant to keep the shot rolling through the screening and mixing steps. It is fed into drumlike grading screens to further standardize the shot sizes. Then it is rolled across a series of triangular-shaped sloping plate glass tables which have had shot rolling across them for more than half a century. At the end of each table is a trench an inch wide. The round shot jump the trench easily and continue through the processing. But any shot that are out-of-round fall into the gap to be remelted.

One of the final steps is a blending process to get the number of shot of a given size per ounce. In the making of No. 6 shot the sizes are mixed with enough No. 6½ shot to give the required 221 pellets per ounce, plus or minus seven shot.

"We do the job the best we know how," Les said. "There is constant quality checking. These towers can turn out twenty thousand pounds of shot an hour. And if we make any mistakes, we just have to melt them down again."

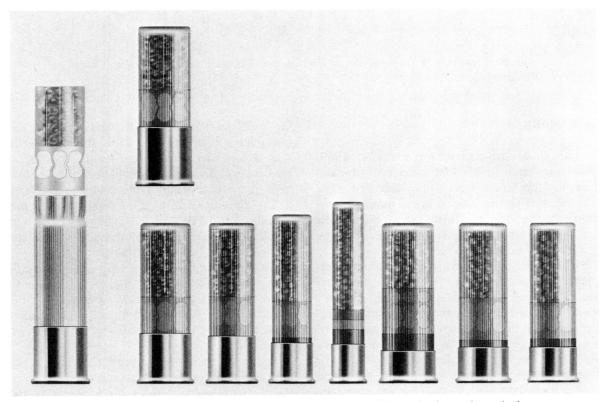

Drawing showing various loads of Remington shells. Note plastic wads and shot-sleeves. *By Remington Arms Co.*

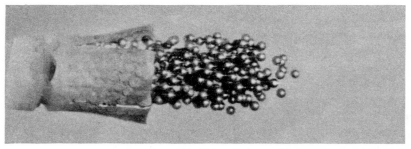

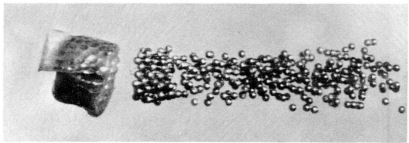

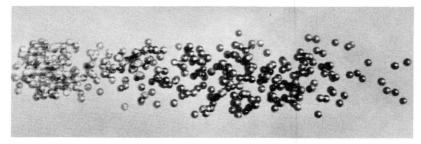

The pictures show a 12-gauge target load of No. 7½ shot as it forms shot string. *By Remington Arms Co.*

Plastic Shells

Plastic shells first came to the market in 1960. Remington Arms was the first to market them, and other manufacturers have since followed. The advantages of plastic include better moisture protection, longer life for those who reload their own, and a tendency to feed into autoloading guns more smoothly.

Plastics have also been replacing other component parts of the shotgun shell in recent years. One interesting development has been the shot sleeve. Shot being pushed through the gun barrel sometimes rub the barrel and are deformed. These shot travel erratically. The plastic shot sleeve fitted into the modern shotgun shell forms a second container for the shot. The exploding powder forces the sleeve, shot and all, from the gun. The plastic falls away behind the shot.

In recent times plastic wads have been replac-ing cellulose and felt wads. Some plastic shot containers or sleeves also form the overpowder wad. Winchester reduced the number of component parts further when it molded its plastic shells to a shape that made a base wad unnecessary.

The development of the crimp wad, which folded the top edges of the casing over like cuts of pie to cover the end of the shell, eliminated the need for a wad over the shot.

No doubt other changes will come in shells. Manufacturers tell me that they could turn out a perfectly good all-plastic case without any brass base, once the shooting public will accept such a shell. Shotgun shells are likely to get better and better.

Today the modern shotgun shell is one of the most reliable commercial products on the store shelves. Anyone who tours an ammunition factory is immediately impressed by the extreme care taken with quality control, testing, and in-

Winchester photograph showing two kinds of crimp: roll crimp (bottom), and pie-shape crimp (top) requiring no overwad. *By Winchester-Western.*

spections. Every step of shell production is inspected. Every completed shell on one typical production line is finally inspected visually two times.

The practical result, from the shooter's point of view, is highly reliable ammunition. The commercially made shell is going to shoot the same as the one before it and the one that follows it because it was produced by highly critical and accurate modern machinery. Hand loaders cannot expect to attain the same degree of standardization.

If you measure the ength of a loaded 2¾-inch shell you will note that it is shorter than 2¾ inches. This is due to the fact that the measurement refers to length before the end is crimped. The gun is chambered for the full length of the uncrimped shell case, however. In this way the case can flatten out as the shell is fired and shot.

Magnums

The term magnum does not necessarily mean a larger shell. It does mean a heavier-than-standard load of shot, and somewhat more powder than carried in standard loads. The reason for shooting magnums is to deliver a heavier pattern of shot at a given range. This makes these big loads especially useful on big birds, such as geese and wild turkeys. For practical purposes the muzzle velocity of standard and magnum loads is about the same.

Magnum shells are factory loaded in both the 2¾- and three-inch sizes. Manufacturers chamber standard guns for 2¾-inch shells. Shotgunners who intend to use three-inch magnums should purchase guns chambered to handle the longer shells. There is nothing wrong with shooting a shell shorter than the gun is chambered for, but it is a mistake—and a hazard—to shoot the three-inch shells in guns chambered for shorter shells.

The shotgunner should not figure that because he chooses a box of magnum loads over the standard loads, he is given any spectacular advantage. The added powder and shot may increase his effective range on flying birds somewhat, simply because of the increased number of pellets. But where the standard field grade 2¾-inch 12-gauge shell may carry 281 No. 6 shot, the magnum 2¾-inch shell will probably contain only an added fifty-seven pellets, or about 20 percent more.

Tracers

One specialized type of shell is the tracer load. Such ammunition has been brought to the market occasionally for many years, dating back beyond World War II. An instructor standing behind the shooter can, with a little practice, see the shot following its path. If the burning materials travel reliably with the shot charge and are clearly visible, the shooter can tell how much he is off

Winchester plastic mark five-shot collar. *By Winchester-Western.*

in figuring his lead, whether he shot above or beneath the target.

The primary use of tracer shells is on shooting clay targets. They have little utility under hunting conditions, and on low shots or short range shots the burning materials might touch off a brush fire.

Brush Loads

A hunter tramping through thick-growing brush for close flushing game would fare better with a shot pattern that opens up at shorter ranges than it might from his choke-bored gun. One answer to this problem, short of changing gun barrels or installing a choke control device, is to carry along some brush or spreader loads. These are offered by the major ammunition manufacturers in 12-, 16-, and 20-gauge sizes. The spreading is accomplished by partitioning the shot into three or four portions with thin dividers.

Rifled Slugs

As I stated in my book *The Deer Hunter's Bible,* any load from a shotgun can kill a deer. This is true no matter how fine the shot, but perhaps the most effective shotgun load ever devised for deer is the rifled slug. This may be disputed in the deer camps of the Southeast because

Winchester cutaway showing shotshell in which base wad is replaced by plastic base as part of the shotshell. *By Winchester-Western.*

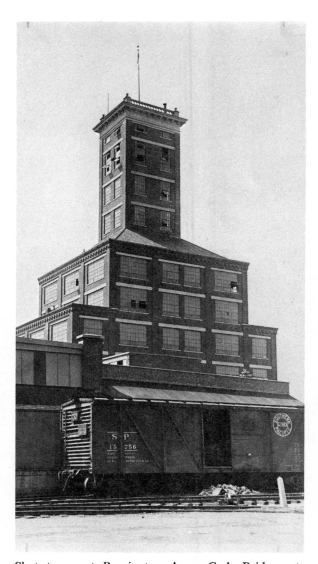

Shot tower at Remington Arms Co.'s Bridgeport, Connecticut ammunition plant. Lead shot rains from top of tower to form and cool. *By Remington Arms Co.*

Bars of lead ready for melting into shot. *By Remington Arms Co.*

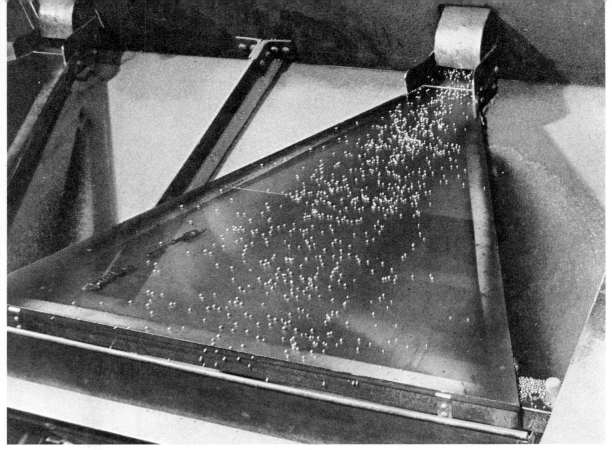

All shot made at Remington shot tower must roll across plate-glass incline. Any shot "out of round" will not jump gap at end of incline, and consequently falls through to be remelted. *By Remington Arms Co.*

Shot pans with proper size holes in bottom are used at top of tower to form shot from molten lead. *By Remington Arms Co.*

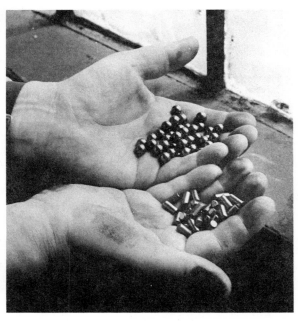

Buckshot is formed from cut cylinders of lead. *By Remington Arms Co.*

there the deer hunter's shotgun is traditionally loaded with buckshot. In thick-growing vegetation, shots usually come at close-up range, a situation where buckshot is highly effective. The rifled slug is better for those longer shots where the shotgun must be used for deer. With a little preseason practice the shotgun handler equipped with rifled slugs can determine how he must aim at various ranges to score.

The rifled slug is a descendant of the round lead ball, but it has seen some refinements in the form of adding lands and grooves in the slug itself. This is designed to make it revolve or spin while traveling its course, instead of tumbling. One other factor in the design of the slug which is credited with keeping it on a true course and preventing tumbling is the fact that it is nose-heavy. At any rate, the modern rifled slug is a highly effective load on large targets. Slugs can be safely shot in guns regardless of how they are bored, even if bored full choke. Guns marketed especially for use with slugs, however, are usually bored cylinder, or without constriction in the muzzle.

Selecting Shot Sizes

Choice of the right size shot for a particular purpose involves a considerable element of personal preference. But the following table can serve as a general guideline because these are shot sizes widely used by experienced hunters.

Kind of Game	Shot Size
Geese	BB, 2, 4
Ducks	4, 5, 6
Wild Turkey	BB, 2, 4
Pheasants	5, 6
Grouse, ruffed	6, 7½, 8
Quail	7½, 8, 9
Doves	7½, 8
Woodcock	7½, 8, 9
Rabbits	5, 6
Squirrels	6, 7½
Rails	7½, 8, 9
Fox	BB, 2, 4
Deer	Buckshot or rifled slug
Black bear	Buckshot or rifled slug

How Many Pellets?

The following information, giving the number of pellets in various shot charges, will prove helpful in patterning the shotgun.

PELLETS PER CHARGE

Shot Size	Ounces of Shot						
	½	¾	⅞	1	1⅛	1¼	1½
9	292	430	512	585	658	731	
8		308	359	410	462	512	
7½	175	263		350	394	438	
6	113	169	197	225	254	281	338
5	85	128	149	170	191	213	
4	68	101	118	135	152	169	203
2			90	102	112	135	

Standard Shot Chart

No.	12	11	10	9	8	7½	6	5	4	2
DIAMETER IN INCHES	.05	.06	.07	.08	.09	.095	.11	.12	.13	.15
APPROXIMATE NUMBER OF PELLETS TO THE OUNCE	2385	1380	870	585	410	350	225	170	135	90

	Air Rifle	BB	No.4 Buck	No.3 Buck	No.1 Buck	No.0 Buck	No.00
DIAMETER IN INCHES	.175	.18	.24	.25	.30	.32	.33
NUMBER TO THE OUNCE / APPROXIMATE NUMBER TO THE POUND	55	50	340	300	175	145	130

Charts showing shot diameter in inches for various shot sizes, and approximate number of pellets per ounce. Also diameters of buckshot and numbers per ounce per pound. *By Winchester-Western.*

Chapter 10

RELOADING

A gunsmith I once knew told of a well-known local shooter who stopped in his shop. "Herb, I reloaded a batch of 12s the other night," he said, "and I have a sneaking feeling I might have got a little extra shot into a couple of them."

Herb has seen them come and go. "I figured right away," he said, "that this guy knew damn well he had heavy loads in some of his shells and he did them that way purposely for some reason. Then he got to fretting about whether or not they might be dangerous, and that's what he was trying to ask me. I told him, 'Throw the whole batch of them away.'"

Two evenings later the same shooter drove up in front of the gun shop again. He was carrying his 12-gauge with him, but he carried it in his right hand because his left hand was in a sling. Fortunately the hand was still intact, and after a while the cuts across it would heal as good as new. The same, however, could never be said for the gun. The breech of the fancy autoloader was ruptured.

"Reloading is perfectly safe," Herb insisted after relating his story, "but not for the shooter who thinks it's all right to tinker around with the recommendations and charts published by the companies that make the powders and components."

Years ago manufacturers began perfecting shells so high in quality that the amateur reloader could seldom match them. These same manufacturers envisioned a society where shooters would be content to stick to the factory loads. Consequently, they were somewhat disillusioned when the age-old interest in reloading failed to fade away. There were fancy and efficient machines brought forth to help shooters who wanted to load their own. Eventually the ammunition manufacturers, to their credit, relaxed and joined the reloaders. They even began marketing all the component parts needed for loading shotshells.

With the ready availability of components and machines to help assemble them plus the growing interest in trap and skeet shooting, there has been a steadily climbing interest in reloading. Most reloaders find this hobby both economically attractive and a pleasant way to pass an occasional evening. The reloaders have organized, and further information on the American Reloading Association may be obtained by writing to them at Box 341, Covina, California 91722.

Because of the army of reloaders, there is seldom a stray empty shell to be found littering the countryside or shooting club grounds. Shooters carefully pick up the shells; many wear low-slung pouches suspended from their belts and drop each spent shell into these carriers. Even officials of the Grand American Trap Shoot collect the shells that shooters do not save. They bag them, then resell the empties to eager purchasers on the last day of the big annual event. I have seen shooters line up a hundred deep, half an hour ahead of the opening of the sales shed where

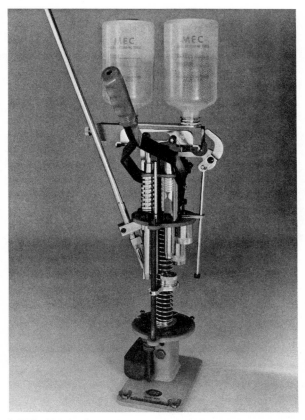

MEC 600 junior reloader available in 10-, 12-, 16-, 20-, 28-, and .410-gauges. *By Mayville Engineering Co.*

the empties are sold after the Grand. In one recent year they paid more than eighteen hundred dollars to get these used shotshells.

While it may be true that the rifleman can actually get more accuracy by reloading his own ammunition, this is seldom the case for the man with the shotgun. He can, however, with proper attention to detail, load shells consistent in their velocities and ballistic characteristics.

Some reloaders practice the art largely because they like to operate machinery, and they want the added satisfaction of firing shells that are products of their own creation. But the fact remains that economy is still the overriding reason accounting for the tremendous growth in hand loading—and a sound reason. Reloading can cut the cost of ammunition approximately in half for a shotgunner.

Although it is possible to invest a lot of money in hand-loading equipment it is not essential, and in some cases unwise. Reloading equipment varies in size from a simple hand kit, selling for about ten dollars, to complex production-line machines which may cost four hundred dollars. It requires no mathematician or professor of economics to tell us that the higher-priced, large-capacity reloading equipment is out of place in the average shooter's home shop. Such reloading equipment is usually purchased by clubs.

My friend Merle Mann, a longtime reloader and gun salesman for the Brendamour's Sporting Goods Stores in Cincinnati, tells me that the average beginning reloader sets himself up in the enterprise for about fifty dollars. "We have one machine," says Merle, "that sells for $33.98 and turns out about 125 shells an hour. We have another one that sells for $179.95 and is capable of turning out 500 shells an hour. Which machine a reloader needs depends upon how much shooting he does. The shotgun owner who shoots a box or two of shells a year would find them pretty expensive if he used either of these machines."

The least expensive equipment I know of that is available for reloading is a highly engineered kit manufactured by Lee Custom Engineering, Inc. of Hartford, Wisconsin. These kits are available in seventy sizes, and a shotgun owner purchases one to match the gauge of his gun. With this equipment each step is a separate hand-loading operation. A bathroom scale can be used to measure pressure. With practice a shooter should be able to reload a box or two of shells in an hour.

With a partially automatic machine operated with a hand lever, the shooter should reload at the rate of 250 shells an hour. Shot and powder reservoirs are usually plastic bottles perched atop the mounted device. The shotshells being loaded move from station to station until they are complete with new primer, powder, wads, shot, and crimp. Such machines are usually capable of reloading only one size shell, and a purchaser must designate the gauge and load wanted. Some, however, are capable of being converted so that more than one gauge of shell can be reloaded with the same machine.

Hydra-MEC. In 12-, 16-, 20-, 28-, and .410-gauges. *By Mayville Engineering Co.*

In addition to the basic reloading equipment, a few accessory items will come in handy. Large sporting goods stores and gun shops stock various kinds of small cabinets and bins which make it possible to store component parts for the reloading process so they are convenient and the possibilities of getting them mixed are reduced. You can also obtain an inexpensive rack for stacking reloads in such a manner that the shell box can be slipped down over each completed batch of twenty-five. Other aids to reloading include an automatic primer tube filler, and primer dispenser.

Components

The task the reloader assigns himself is replacing in the empty shell each of the component parts removed from it when he fired the shell, and putting them there in the order and in such a manner as to give him the desired ballistic results. A list of the component parts required would include primers, powder, shot, empty shell tubes, and wads. Most reloaders now also use polyethylene shot columns which may or may not be combined with the overpowder wad. These can be purchased at gun shops and sporting goods stores. Available also in the stores are new shotshell cases either empty or already primed. Reloaders can purchase shotgun shells in 12 and other gauges, which in lots of one hundred sell at between five and seven cents each. The price of plastic, combination shot column, and wad is about twelve dollars per thousand. Primers used for reloading shotgun shells usually cost about a cent and a half each in lots of one thousand.

The choice of component parts for the home manufacture of shotgun shells is extremely wide, and the possibilities for error in combining them are infinite. This makes it essential to study carefully the charge data and charts before beginning.

Obviously, there are hazards involved in the handling of any flammable or explosive material such as primers and gunpowder. The danger, however, is less than many people consider it to be. Gunpowders come in sealed, approved canisters, clearly labeled. Manufacturers, although quick to point out the hazards of working with gunpowder, sometimes also point out that it is less dangerous than such materials as gasoline and cleaning fluids. Gunpowder will burn, and should be kept away from heat and open flames. The reloader should never smoke while handling gunpowder. He reduces the possibility of carelessly made mistakes by not permitting himself to be distracted by outside influences while busy at his reloading bench. Powders should be stored in a cool, dry place, in their original containers. Never mix one with the other, and never use at all when there is any doubt about their identity. If for some reason you want to dispose of a lot of gunpowder, mix it half and half with earth and spread it on the ground.

Dram Equivalent

It is still common in this age of smokeless powder to see the term "dram equivalent." This term does not mean a measure of weight or volume. In times past, the amount of black powder used to charge a shell was measured in drams—the unit of weight. The newer smokeless powders, however, were far more powerful, dram for dram. Much less of the smokeless powder

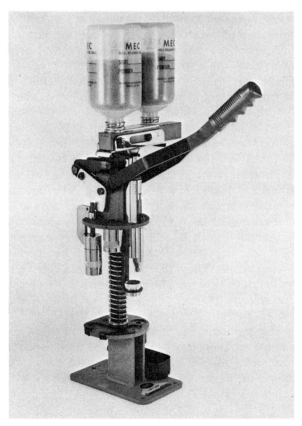

MEC650 Progressive Reloader. Capacity about six hundred plastic reloads per hour. *By Mayville Engineering Co.*

was required to move a shot charge at a speed equivalent to that delivered by a dram of black powder. The term "dram equivalent" refers to equivalent velocities.

Good patterns result, in part, from pressure of the burning powder peaking at the right instant. Ballistic experimentation reveals that poor patterns can result from selecting the wrong powder or wad for the job.

If you check the patterns of your reloads and find that you are getting amazingly good ones, you may be obtaining them at the sacrifice of velocity. An early indicator of a low-velocity shot charge may be that your shotgun "kicks" less than it does with comparable factory loads. Look for the trouble in the primer, the loss of gas pressure around improperly fitting wads, or a charge of powder that is too light.

There is a considerable hazard in overloading a shell either with too much shot or too much powder. Increasing a load of shot, even by a fraction of an ounce, without corresponding changes in the other components may dangerously increase the breech pressure in the gun. A similar result may come from the use of a powder that burns too fast. And an improper wad used in a load can also create high breech pressure. Shells that deliver more than a normal amount of apparent recoil may be developing too much breech pressure. Alcan Company, Inc. of Alcan, Illinois, manufacturer of shotgun shells as well as powders and other components, supplies a ballistics analysis service which might be helpful to hand loaders confronted with serious questions about the loads they assemble. To take advantage of this service, hand loaders send six shells and six dollars to Alcan. All loaded ammunition, incidentally, must be shipped by railway express. First, one is disassembled in the laboratory for a close look. Then the other five are test-fired by ballistics experts. The report rendered includes the velocity in feet per second as well as the breech pressure created by the shells.

The handling of primers calls for a certain amount of caution. They should be stored under cool, dry conditions. High temperatures or a hard blow will sometimes explode a primer, and it can inflict wounds.

Shotshells

What do you do with all those empty shotshells you gather up and bring back from a trap or skeet range? The collection may include a mixture from various manufacturers and different types of shells. There may be both plastic and paper cases. Some may be in perfect condition for reloading; others may be unsuitable for further use. Until you are ready to begin reloading them, the cases should be stored in some clean, dry place.

Step one in reloading consists of sorting the shells and checking them for condition. Every shell has an inner base wad. One of its functions is to fill space, thus allowing the proper space for the components. It is possible in the firing of a shell to damage the inner base wad, and this could alter the powder load. Consequently, it becomes important to measure the inner base wad before reloading the shell. Any reloader can make a gauge for this by setting a small stick into an empty shell of the same make and style and marking the point reached on the stick by the open end of the shell case. Those that vary in depth from the marked dowel when measured before reloading should be discarded.

Base wad condition is important. Shells with base wads damaged by burning should not be reloaded.

The height of the brass at the base of the shell, incidentally, has little if any relationship to the height of the inner base wad. In fact, on some modern, strong plastic shells the brass cup on the outside has no real function, except to satisfy the demands of the purchaser who is accustomed to seeing brass on the outside of shells. Any shells seriously dented or bent should be discarded. Shells that have been previously reloaded and are too weak at the open end to crimp should also be discarded. The reloading procedure can be summarized in eight steps.

1. Decapping. This step consists of punching out the old fired primer.
2. Priming. The primer has to be replaced with a new one charged with a nonmercuric compound.
3. Charging Powder. With most hand loaders a fixed amount of powder is measured and dropped automatically.
4. Seating Wads. The old-style paper felt and cork wads have largely gone the way of black powder and the flintlock. Modern reloaders almost always select plastic over powder wads. In addition to the pressing and holding of powder in place the wad must act as a gas seal and must also cushion the shot.

Depriming.

Replacing primer.

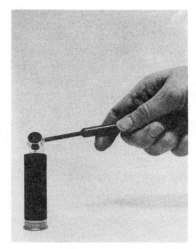

Loading measured powder.

Inserting wads.

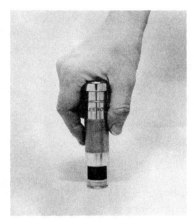

Seating wads.

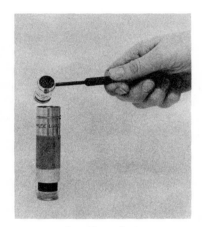

Loading shot.

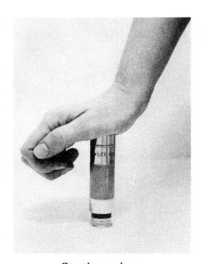

Starting crimp.

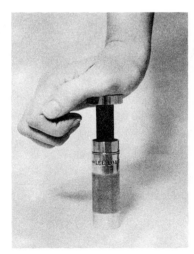

Completing crimp.

Ejecting shell.

Series showing steps involved in reloading shell with Lee loader. *By Lee Custom Engineering Co.*

5. Charging Shot. The shot is measured automatically in most reloading machines.

6. Crimp Starting. Because plastic shells are more difficult to crimp than paper shells, crimping is commonly done in two stages.

7. Crimping. In this stage a die in the machine completes the closure of the shotshell.

8. Resizing. This final operation assures the reloader that his loaded shell does not bulge where it shouldn't and is reshaped to fit the chamber of his gun. With most reloading equipment the steps are not accomplished as separate hand operations, but are done in semiautomatic fashion by the machine itself, moving shells from station to station.

In some equipment. the reloader has only to place empty shells on the rotating table of the device, pull the lever, and remove filled shells from the last station.

Powder

The following guide lists popular powders available for reloading shotshells. This information, supplied by the manufacturers, should enable a shooter to choose a powder suitable for his gun and type of shooting.

DUPONT POWDERS

PB Powder This powder, available in one-half pound, four-pound, or twenty-five-pound quantities, gives a three-dram equivalent velocity at relatively low chamber pressures. The manufacturer considers it best suited to the reloading of 20- and 28-gauge target loads. It can also be used in 12-gauge target loads.

SR4756 Powder The manufacturer recommends this powder for target reloads in 20- and 28-gauge as well as for magnum-type reloads. It is available in one-half pound canisters, four-pound caddies, and twenty-five-pound drums.

HI-SKOR 700-X Designed for modern 12-gauge components, this popular powder is said to give optimum ballistic results with minimum charge weights. It is a dense, double-base powder for which the wad pressures are not highly critical.

SR7625 Powder This powder is designed for reloading 12-gauge, high-velocity "duck loads." It is available in one-half pound, four-pound, and twenty-five-pound lots.

IMR4227 Powder This is the powder often selected for reloading .4104 shotshell ammunition. It comes in one-pound canisters and eight- and twenty-pound kegs.

HERCULES POWDERS

Green Dot This powder, available in eight-ounce, three-pound, and twelve-pound quantities, is designed primarily for use in reloading 12-gauge medium-shotshell loads.

Herco A coarse-grained shotgun powder for use in reloading magnums and heavy shotshell loads. It can be purchased in ten-ounce canisters, and four- and fifteen-pound kegs.

Hercules 2400 This powder is useful in reloading .410-bore shotshells. It is a fine-grained powder available in one- and five-pound quantities.

Red Dot Popular among reloaders, this powder is widely used for light and standard shotshell loading. It comes in eight-ounce canisters and three- and twelve-pound kegs.

Unique Intended as an all-around powder, this one is useful in reloading pistol and rifle cartridges as well as for a variety of shotshell loads. It is packaged in thirteen-ounce canisters and four- and fifteen-pound kegs.

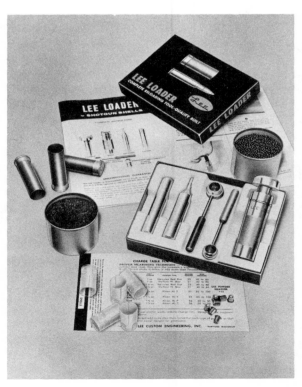

Inexpensive reloading kit. Price about ten dollars. *By Lee Custom Engineering Company.*

Lyman Easy Shotshell Reloader handles paper, brass, zinc, and plastic cases. Adaptable to all gauges. Loads all shell lengths. Reloads average 240 shells per hour. *By Lyman Gun Sight Corp.*

ALCAN POWDERS

AL-5 This powder, as well as other Alcan powders mentioned here, was developed solely for reloading. AL-5 is a dense, progressively burning shotgun powder designed for heavy loads. This powder and the following two are packed in eight-ounce and three- and six-pound kegs.

AL-7 Designed for magnum loads with heavy shot charges. This is a dense, progressively burning powder.

AL-8 This coarse-grained powder should be used only with heavy maximum loads.

AL-120 This one was especially designed for general use in trap and field loads. It is available in various quantities, ranging from half-pound tins to twenty-four-pound kegs.

10-GAUGE

Shell	Shot Charge (oz.)	Velocity	Powder Type	Grains Powder Paper Wad	Grains Powder Plastic Wad	Wad Pressure
10-ga.	1¼	1300	AL-120	37.0	34.0	50
2⅞″	1¼	1335	AL-5	41.0	38.0	50
	1¼	1360	Green Dot	33.0	31.0	50
	1¼	1360	Red Dot	31.0	29.0	50
	1¼	1360	Herco	44.0	42.0	100
	1¼	1360	Unique	31.0	29.0	50
	1¼	1310	700X	27.0	24.0	none
	1¼	1350	DuPont PB	35.0	30.0	90
	1⅝	1330	AL-5	44.0	41.0	50
	1⅝	1330	Green Dot	34.0	32.0	50
	1⅝	1330	Red Dot	32.0	30.0	50
	1⅝	1330	Herco	45.0	43.0	100
	1⅝	1330	Unique	32.0	30.0	50
	1⅝	1330	500HS	43.5	41.0	70
	1¾	1245	SR4756	43.0	39.0	100
10-ga.	2	1330	Green Dot	35.0	33.0	50
3½″	2	1330	Red Dot	33.0	31.0	50
MAG.	2	1330	Herco	46.0	44.0	100
	2	1330	Unique	33.0	31.0	50
	2	1205	SR4756	45.0	41.0	100
	2	1330	540MS	56.0	51.0	70
	2	1330	AL-7	49.0	44.0	50
	2	1335	AL-8	59.0	54.0	50
	2¼	1250	AL-8	58.0	52.0	50

Courtesy *Lee Reloading Handbook*
and DuPont, Hercules, Alcan, Olin.

12-GAUGE

Shell	Shot Charge (oz.)	Velocity	Powder Type	Grains Powder Paper Wad	Grains Powder Plastic Wad	Wad Pressure
12-ga.	1	1235	AL-120	24.0	23.0	50
2¾″	1	1235	Red Dot	21.0	19.0	50
	1	1235	Green Dot	23.0	22.0	50
	1	1235	Unique	23.0	22.0	50
	1	1200	700X	21.0	19.0	none
	1	1200	DuPont PB	25.0	23.0	40
	1	1235	450LS	25.0	24.0	70
Trap	1⅛	1200	AL-120	24.0	23.0	50
and	1⅛	1200	Red Dot	22.0	20.0	50
Skeet	1⅛	1200	Green Dot	23.0	22.0	50
	1⅛	1200	Unique	23.0	22.0	50
	1⅛	1200	700X	21.0	20.0	none
	1⅛	1200	DuPont PB	25.0	23.0	50
	1⅛	1200	450LS	23.5	21.0	40
Field	1¼	1330	AL-5	34.0	31.0	50
Loads	1¼	1220	Green Dot	24.0	23.0	50
	1¼	1330	Herco	31.0	29.0	100
	1¼	1330	Unique	25.0	24.0	50
	1¼	1200	DuPont PB	27.0	25.0	40
	1¼	1330	500HS	25.5	30.0	40
12-ga.	1⅜	1325	AL-7	37.0	34.0	50
2¾″	1⅜	1340	Herco	32.0	30.0	100
MAG	1⅜	1315	500HS	37.0	32.0	40
	1½	1320	AL-7	37.0	34.0	50
	1½	1315	Herco	32.0	30.0	100
	1½	1255	SR4756	37.0	35.0	70
12-ga.	1⅝	1300	AL-7	37.0	33.0	50
3″	1⅝	1315	Herco	36.0	34.0	100
MAG.	1¾	1265	AL-8	46.0	41.0	50
	1⅞	1255	540MS	39.0	36.0	40

Courtesy *Lee Reloading Handbook*
and DuPont, Hercules, Alcan, Olin.

16-GAUGE

Shell	Shot Charge (oz.)	Velocity	Powder Type	Grains Powder Paper Wad	Grains Powder Plastic Wad	Wad Pressure
16-ga.	⅞	1250	AL-120	21.0	20.0	40
2¾″	⅞	1205	700X	17.0	16.0	none
	1	1200	AL-120	20.0	19.0	40
	1	1200	Green Dot	18.5	17.5	50
	1	1165	Red Dot	17.0	16.0	50
	1	1200	Red Dot	18.0	17.0	50
	1	1200	Unique	19.5	18.5	50
	1	1165	450LS	19.0	18.0	70
	1	1135	DuPont PB	19.0	18.0	none
	1	1220	AL-5	26.0	23.0	40
	1	1140	700X	16.0	15.0	none
	1⅛	1200	AL-7	28.0	25.0	40
	1⅛	1240	Unique	21.0	20.0	50
	1⅛	1295	Unique	22.0	21.0	50
	1⅛	1295	Herco	26.0	24.0	100
	1⅛	1185	500HS	23.0	21.0	70
	1⅛	1295	540MS	31.0	28.0	70
	1⅛	1300	SR4756	28.0	25.0	none
16-ga.	1¼	1265	AL-8	36.0	33.0	40
2¾″	1¼	1260	540MS	30.0	27.0	70
MAG.	1¼	1200	SR4756	27.5	25.0	none

Courtesy *Lee Reloading Handbook*
and DuPont, Hercules, Alcan, Olin.

20-GAUGE

Shell	Shot Charge (oz.)	Velocity	Powder Type	Grains Powder Paper Wad	Grains Powder Plastic Wad	Wad Pressure
20-ga.	¾	1100	700X	15.0	13.0	none
2¾″	¾	1230	AL-120	17.0	16.0	40
	⅞	1200	AL-120	18.0	17.0	40
	⅞	1220	AL-5	24.0	22.0	40
	⅞	1155	Unique	17.0	16.0	40
	⅞	1200	Green Dot	18.0	17.0	40
	⅞	1200	Red Dot	17.5	16.0	40
	⅞	1145	DuPont PB	18.0	17.0	40
	⅞	1315	SR4756	27.0	25.0	40
	⅞	1155	450LS	16.0	15.0	40
	1	1220	AL-7	25.0	22.0	40
	1	1220	Herco	20.0	18.0	60
	1	1220	Unique	19.0	18.0	40
	1	1200	SR4756	27.0	23.0	30
	1	1165	500HS	20.0	18.0	40
	1	1220	540MS	25.0	22.0	40

20-GAUGE (cont.)

Shell	Shot Charge (oz.)	Velocity	Powder Type	Grains Powder Paper Wad	Grains Powder Plastic Wad	Wad Pressure
20-ga.	1⅛	1220	Herco	21.0	19.0	60
2¾″	1⅛	1260	AL-8	32.0	30.0	40
MAG.	1⅛	1220	540MS	25.0	22.0	60
	1⅛	1100	SR4756	24.0	21.0	40
20-ga.	1³⁄₁₆	1250	AL-8	33.0	30.0	40
3″	1¼	1150	Hcl.2400	37.0	33.0	60
	1¼	1160	IMR4227	44.0	41.0	25

Courtesy *Lee Reloading Handbook*
and DuPont, Hercules, Alcan, Olin.

.410-GAUGE

Shell	Shot Charge (oz.)	Velocity	Powder Type	Grains Powder Paper Wad	Grains Powder Plastic Wad	Wad Pressure
.410-ga.	⅜	1150	AL-8	12.0	no	25
2½″	½	1140	Hcl.2400	15.0	information	25
	½	1155	IMR4227	18.0	available	25
.410-ga.	⅝	1050	Hcl.2400	15.5	no	25
3″	⅝	1125	IMR4227	18.0	information	none
	¾	1050	Hcl.2400	16.0	available	25

Courtesy *Lee Reloading Handbook*
and DuPont, Hercules, Alcan, Olin.

SHOT			
Oz. of Shot per Shell	Shells from 5 Lb.	Shells from 25 Lb.	Shells from 100 Lb.
⅜	213	1067	4268
½	174	872	3490
⅝	128	640	2560
¾	106	533	2134
⅞	91	457	1830
1	80	400	1600
1 1/16	75	376	1506
1⅛	71	355	1422
1 3/16	67	336	1346
1¼	64	320	1280
1⅜	58	291	1164
1½	53	266	1066
1⅝	49	246	984
1¾	45	228	914
1⅞	42	213	854
2	40	200	800
2¼	35	178	712

Courtesy *Alcan Reloader's Manual.*

STANDARD SHOT		
Shot Size	Diameter	Approx. Number per Oz.
Fine Dust	.03	
Dust	.04	4565
No. 12	.05	2330
11	.06	1350
10	.07	850
9	.08	570
8	.09	400
7½	.095	340
6	.11	220
5	.12	170
4	.13	135
3	.14	105
2	.15	85
1	.16	70
B	.17	60
BB	.18	50
BBB	.19	42

Courtesy *Alcan Reloader's Manual.*

POWDER			
Grs. of Powder per Shell	Shells from 8 Oz.	Shells from 1 Lb.	Shells from 3 Lb.
16	218	437	1311
18	194	388	1164
19	184	368	1104
21	166	333	999
22	159	318	954
23	152	304	912
24	145	291	873
25	140	280	840
26	132	265	795
27	129	259	777
28	125	250	750
29	120	241	723
30	116	233	699
32	109	218	654
33	106	212	636
34	102	205	615
37	94	189	567
38	92	184	552
39	89	179	537
50	70	140	420
52	68	136	409
54	64	129	388
56	62	125	375
58	60	121	362

Courtesy *Alcan Reloader's Manual.*

Chapter 11

HOW TO SHOOT BETTER

Every shotgun handler everywhere—from the beginner who has yet to fire his first hundred rounds to the old-time trap shooter who has long since lost track—has one thing in common: he wants to shoot better than he does. At first glance it would seem relatively easy. Out there in front of you is a moving target. In your hands is an instrument that throws not a single projectile but perhaps as many as several hundred pellets. It creates a pattern of shot only a small portion of which must score to break a target or take the game. It seems simple enough—until you miss.

In shooting, as in golf, basketball, or a long list of other activities, the best beginning is with sound coaching. Most shooters are self-taught. The self-taught, however, learn from teachers who are poorly informed. Quite often starting to shoot without guidance instills bad habits in a shooter—habits he must shed later if he is to become a first-rate shooter. There are, of course, a few good shooters who display poor form and employ methods that make the classic shotgun handler wonder how they can get away with it. But they are good in spite of the way they shoot, and they may never know whether they would be better shots if they had learned the right principles from the beginning.

In the belief that good shooting begins with expert coaching, I recently observed Ken Berger, Remington field representative and one of the country's top shotgun handlers, giving basic instruction to a husky teen-age high school student whose shooting experience had been limited. We were standing on the sixteen-yard line behind one of the trap houses of the Latonia Gun Club in the hills of northern Kentucky.

"The first thing to think about," Ken explained, "is your stance. You've played basketball? Good. You know how you should stand when you're ready to make a shot. It's the same with a shotgun. The left foot should be forward. The feet should be far enough apart to be comfortable, about a foot apart. The toe of the left foot should point about forty-five degrees to the right of where you think the target will come from.

"Your weight should be largely on the forward foot. If you were a left-hand shooter it would be the other way—the right foot would be forward."

Until this point the student had held the gun at waist level. "Now let me see you mount the gun," Ken said.

As experienced shooters realize, having the head, which means the right eye or sighting eye, in even a slightly wrong position as you look across the gun barrel can mean a miss by yards of blue sky. The gun should come up to the shoulder smoothly, and it should come all the way into position. You know when it's in position by the fact that your cheek is in place on the comb without lowering the head. It is not a case of getting the sighting eye lined up along the sights, as you might with a rifle. In fact, there is very little about rifle shooting that can be transferred to the shotgun, and the transition is sometimes difficult for the practiced rifleman.

Ken began at this point to review the beginner's shooting form point by point. First was the position of the left hand in which the forearm of the 12-gauge rested. The shooter, he suggested, should extend the forefinger along the gunstock, as if he were pointing at the target. The shotgun is pointed from the eye to the target.

The correct position for the left hand on the gun's forearm should be a point comfortable to the shooter. The hand should come to the same place on the gun every time. Some tournament shooters mark the forearm of their gun at the point where the fingers should rest. This keeps the left hand from drifting out of position in the excitement and tension of competition. You may be able to speed up your swing by moving your hand back.

The right shoulder should come up slightly so the gunstock will be shouldered at the right height in relation to the eye. The right elbow should not be too high—a fault that rifle shooters sometimes bring to shotgun shooting. "The whole idea," Ken explained, "is to shoot in a position that is comfortable."

Once good shooting form has been learned, consistency is essential. The gunstock must come to the same place on the shoulder and against the cheek with every shot. And the stock should come to the face, not the face to the stock. Shooters sometimes tend to lift the head slightly

Experienced trap shooter giving tips to beginning shotgunner, emphasizing the importance of proper stance and balance. Feet should be spread comfortably with most of the weight on the forward foot. *By George Laycock.*

as they shoot. Thinking about this, one realizes that the eye and the muzzle of the gun mark two points on a straight line. Ideally, this line is pointing at the target. Lifting the eye—which is one of the points on the line—but a fraction of an inch creates a new line of sight. Properly placed, the eye does not see much of the gun barrel. It is looking at the target in relation to the end of the barrel.

By this time the student knew how to shoulder his gun properly. He was leaning slightly forward, his weight on his left foot. "Now let's try a few shots." From his position behind the student's shoulder, Ken could look down the gun barrel.

"Remember," he said, "that you don't aim— you point. You point with the muzzle."

Some people think of the shot as going out

there in a flat wall, but it doesn't. Instead, it spreads out in a string. Not all the shot arrive at the same time. You want to put the shot where the target will fly into the shot string.

Before letting his student call for the first bird, Ken passed along a couple of other pointers. He checked the trigger finger. "You don't squeeze the trigger of a shotgun," he said, "the way a rifleman does. Instead, get the gun up and on target and slap or pull the trigger. Just the tip of your finger should be on the trigger. Grip the gun firmly enough to maintain good control and don't let the trigger finger touch anything but the trigger.

"You shooting with one or both eyes open?"

"Both," the student replied.

Closing one eye is a disadvantage with which many beginning shooters saddle themselves. Learn from the first to shoot every time with both eyes open, because you can watch the target better. In any event only one eye—the master eye—lines up the target. For most people the master eye is the right eye. This is easily verified. You may have noticed that if you look along your extended arm and forefinger and close one eye at a time, the finger seems to jump aside for one eye, but remains in place for the other. Point at some object across the room. Close one eye. If the finger held on its aiming point, the open eye is your master eye. If it "jumps" to one side, the other eye is your master eye. It is the master eye that should be looking along the gun barrel.

Actually, there is but a single good method of hitting fast-moving targets. Swing the gun to track the target, overtake it, and snap the trigger at the point which will send the pattern of shot out at the right instant and in the right place to intercept the target. This swing and follow-through method is basic. It should be a smooth action that gets the shooter on his target fast. Experience will tell him when to get the shot off. "I want you to think of it as if you're swinging a paint brush," Ken said, "and you're going to paint over the target. When you've painted it out, shoot."

Those who shoot flying targets soon understand the importance of leading the targets or getting ahead of them with the string of shot. One occasionally sees tables of accepted lead distances for various kinds of targets, from clay targets on the skeet range to flying ducks, doves,

pheasants, and quail. These leads cannot be more than relative estimates. A shooter must learn largely by experience how much to lead a target. On a straightaway shot he knows to cover the target point-blank. He learns to lead both horizontally and vertically on targets angling away, and gaining or losing altitude. A duck flying against the wind is likely to require less lead than the same bird with the wind in his tail. Slow-flying birds obviously call for less lead than the fast fliers.

When the student called for his first bird, the clay target sailed out of the trap house going away to the left. He swung on it, let it go a bit too far, and missed. "Do you know where the gun muzzle was in relation to the target when you fired?" The student admitted, as he thought it through, that he had a poor idea of the relationship of the gun to the target. "Try it again," Ken said.

The boy missed the target again, but he was beginning to understand why. "I think I shot below it."

There is a time lag between the time you decide to shoot and the time it takes the shooter and the gun to react. "More than one factor figures into this," Ken added. "One is your reaction time. Then there is the speed with which you swing the gun. And some guns have slower mechanisms than others. It's difficult to tell a person how much to lead a bird. On the rising shots it's best to shoot a little above the target; on the falling birds, a little below. I shoot as soon as my swing overtakes the bird with the muzzle of the gun.

"But this brings in the matter of follow-through," he explained. "If you shoot, then stop the gun's swing, the time lag is going to put the shot where you're pointing long after the bird has gone. Follow through just as you would in golf. Then the speed of the swing will help take care of the lead problem, especially at close range."

His student continued to call for birds and to fire on them. He scored with increasing frequency. They also worked together analyzing both the hits and misses. There were times when the boy was hesitant and slow to get on the target. "You have to get right on it," Ken explained, "and fire as soon as you're on the target. It's a positive procedure, quick and with authority—not pokey. Don't stop to think it through. Try shooting without worrying about your feet, hands, or anything else except painting out that target with the muzzle of your gun. If I see that you are doing anything wrong, we'll talk about it. Otherwise, just keep your eyes on the target. Concentrate on the target."

Ken also explained that the experienced shooter often knows how he shot by what happens to a clay target. When the student "smoked" one, Ken explained that the first shot in the string broke the target, and the rest of the following pellets powdered the pieces as they fell into the string.

One shot sent a few fragments of the clay target in one direction but tumbled the largest fragment downward. "You know why the big part went down? Because your shot was a little high. If the big fragment goes up, you have shot a little lower than you should. If the big part goes to the left, you shot too far to the right, which on a bird quartering to the left would mean you were shooting behind the target. If the big part goes to the right on the same bird, you would be shooting a little too far to the left or ahead of it. Remembering this can help you correct your shooting."

Tension and emotion play a part in how well a shooter performs, as any seasoned tournament shooter will assure you. Every shooter has his good and his bad days. If he is worried about other matters, it can show up in poor scores. If the pressure of the match grows, the shooter may begin missing.

Ken and other experienced shooters agree that some people develop into good shooters more easily than others. Some become better golfers, tennis players, or archers than others. Shooters differ in their athletic abilities and reaction speeds. But shooting ability is not something you are born with or without. This is why even the excellent shots have to practice so much.

Shooting skill comes with firing a lot of shells. But it comes sooner to those who start with the help of a good instructor.

Remington professional Ken Berger instructing beginner. Good coaching is important and helps to develop good shooting habits from the start. The aim is to put the shot string where the target will fly into it. Some coaches suggest using shotguns as paintbrush and "painting out" target. *By George Laycock.*

Chapter 12

TRAPS AND TARGETS

We are assured by those who enjoy exploring musty records that the history of target shooting is a long, and, generally speaking, honorable one, reaching back beyond the birth of firearms. An ancient poet of three thousand years ago tells us that archers of the time sharpened their aim on captive doves.

Organized shooting at moving targets was under way in England before it caught on in North America. In the early 1800s the gentry began keeping in practice by shooting live pigeons. Then some ingenious soul stuck a pigeon beneath his top hat and announced that he would straightaway release the bird, replace his hat, then shoot—which would give the bird a bit of a sporting chance.

The idea grew, and clubs of shooters organized to take up the strange practice. Some tell us the first such club was called the High Hats; others claim it was the "Old Hats."

At any rate, the shooters must have tired of having pigeons soil their pates, because the game soon gave way to one in which pigeons were placed on the ground beneath the old hats. To each such hat a string was attached. At the proper moment the string was pulled. The hat tumbled over, the bird flew, and the gunner shot him—sometimes. This was the birth of trap shooting.

Top hats were destined to give way to box traps with hinged lids. Such traps held the pigeons until the string could be pulled to release them. In parts of the world where live pigeon shoots are still permitted, the traps are scarcely different in principle than were those early models.

Trap shooting in the United States apparently had its beginning in 1831. That year the Sportsman's Club in Cincinnati, Ohio held a live pigeon shoot.

But with advancing civilization and maturing standards, the days of using live birds for target practice were numbered. Even the house sparrows once live-trapped and shipped around the Midwest were to be protected from this fate. Inanimate targets were to replace them.

The change to inanimate targets probably began, as one authority speculates, with one shooter's tossing up potatoes or apples for the other. The first inanimate targets especially made for the purpose were glass balls. These ancestors of clay targets were slightly more than two inches in diameter. This was in 1866, in Boston. The trap used to propel the glass targets was a spring affair that tossed the sphere straight up.

Some inventors went a step farther. In an effort to make the shooting realistic, they filled the glass balls with chicken feathers, which drifted down on the breeze when a shooter scored. Some glass balls were filled with smoke.

The search for a perfect target continued. One inventor tried a small rubber balloon that could be fitted into a cardboard disk. Others even tried fitting balloons into metal frames made in the shape of pigeons. One pellet was enough to bring such a "bird" to the ground. Perhaps the fanciest of these was created in England. It came sliding in on a wire with its wings flapping, and if the shooter failed to hit it, the creation went riding on out with its wings still flapping. But should he catch the target in the pattern of shot, the balloon burst and the wings stopped flapping, which is about what one would expect to happen to any bird with a burst balloon.

But all these flights of fancy were going a little farther than needed. By 1880 a Cincinnatian named George Ligowsky had invented the baked clay target, and it looked quite similar to the ones still being thrown today. The only trouble was that they were so hard they seldom broke when hit. Then composition targets came

Clay targets, easily shattered by shot string, have long history in shooting sports and have now been standardized in dimensions. *By Remington Arms Co.*

along, and since that time, 1884, there have been few further improvements in targets. The standard clay target today is 4¼ inches in diameter. They are widely available at a few dollars for a carton of 135.

Hand Traps

Every year as summer wears on and the first days of the hunting season approach, dedicated gunners dig out their hand traps and clay targets. They're off for some valuable practice with the simplest of all devices made to propel clay birds.

The hand trap is a portable device with a spring and cocking mechanism and metal fingers or a tray for holding circular clay targets. A person can, with a little practice, learn to bring the hand trap forward with a motion that releases the spring and sends the target hurtling out and away. And with a little more practice he becomes capable of throwing targets as tricky as a gunner will encounter anywhere.

There are at least five advantages favoring the hand trap. It is inexpensive. Any one of several models can be purchased at sporting goods stores for five dollars or less. In addition, it is easily carried, and so small that it requires scarcely any storage space. It can be kept in the back of a car or pickup truck along with a supply of

targets, and the shooter is ready for a practice session any time. Also, the hand trap is versatile. It will throw targets to duplicate all kinds of shots a gunner might have. It will send high-flying "birds" straight up or scoot a ground-skimming target off into the thicket. Using a hand trap is fun. And finally, it is excellent practice for the coming hunting trips. These reasons together add up to strong arguments in favor of every shooting family's owning a hand trap.

Most hand traps are built to handle single targets. But those who want to practice shooting doubles can obtain hand traps with trays or grips for holding two targets.

The use of a hand trap calls for the cooperation of two or more shooters. One throws the targets while his companion shoots. They take turns throwing and shooting. I have seen agile gunners throw their own targets with a hand trap, drop the trap, shoulder the gun, and score. But this grows old fast, and it lacks the companionship element important to many shooting games.

Over the years shooters have worked out a great variety of games in which hand traps are employed. Some practice for the coming waterfowl season by shooting clay targets from

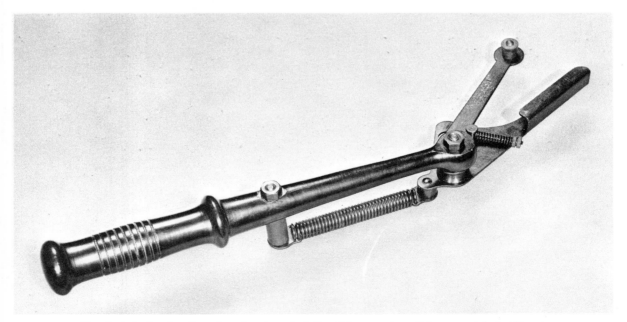

Simplest device for throwing clay targets is hand trap such as this one made by Remington. Great variety of shots are possible with targets thrown from this trap. *By Remington Arms Co.*

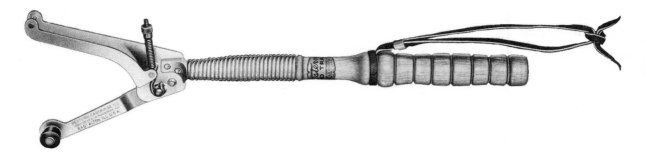

Hand trap made by Olin Industries, Inc. *By Winchester-Western.*

Hunting partners can take turns throwing targets for each other while walking through variety of cover and in this manner simulate shots they might encounter on live game. *By Erwin A. Bauer.*

cramped duck blinds. The target thrower can work from either side of the blind and take the gunner by surprise with the various angles at which the birds come. Or those who really want to test their skill can have two friends throw double targets from either side of the blind at about the same time.

Upland bird hunters often walk through cover similar to that which they hunt, while their companion comes along behind and to one side with the hand trap. His aim is to take the shooter by surprise—which is no more than the live bird might do.

Shooters should have little trouble finding a place to shoot with a hand trap. There must be at least three hundred yards of open country in front of the shooter. Farmers will frequently not object to practice sessions on their land, and the land owner might like to join in the shooting. One thing to remember is that the broken clay targets will be picked up and eaten by hogs if the animals have access to them—and they are poisonous to hogs. So choose practice places where everyone, man and pig alike, is safe from danger.

One step beyond the hand traps are the economically priced spring-operated mechanical traps which propel targets from fixed positions. In 1956 George Luebkeman, another Cincinnatian, decided to make and market the first light, portable trap capable of throwing doubles. He had been a shooter since he was old enough to hold a shotgun. Although he doesn't recall the details, George went on his first hunting trip at the age of six weeks. With his mother and father he slept that night in a hay mow. Wisconsin's spring duck season had just come in. Before daylight the next morning the Luebkemans, including little George, were in the duck blind. Understandably, George had ample opportunity through the years to learn about guns. Eventually he became an ardent shooter, and international skeet became his favorite target sport.

One day recently I stopped by George's little factory. "Let's go out and do some shooting," he said. "We have a place over here where we practice." Shortly we were throwing clay birds for each other, and George was showing me various methods by which one or two shooters—or more—can set up such a trap for shooting.

"One of the good ways," he said, "is to mount the base on a long board so you can drive one

wheel of your car over the end of the board. Another idea that is perhaps the best of all is to mount it on the top of a fifty-five-gallon steel oil drum."

These lightweight traps are also equipped with metal augers which anchor them to the ground.

After we had thrown clay targets for a while, George began trying other targets. "It works well for tin cans," he said. "We have this little metal attachment to hold the cans." He attached a flat piece of metal with two bolts, then loaded the trap with a quart oil can. "Trip it," he said.

I pulled the string, and the can went hurtling off through the air. At about thirty-five yards George peppered it with No. 8 shot. Next he tried corncobs, and those worked well too. "Anything like that is a potential target," he said, "but I can't see where it makes much sense to economize this much on targets when you're shooting shells that cost ten cents each. You'll not find a better inanimate target anyhow than the clay birds we have today."

Gun Clubs

Some years ago nine friends who live and hunt in the vicinity of Union, Ohio, not far

Shooting games using hand traps and clay targets make excellent family-type activity. *By Erwin A. Bauer.*

Even on hunting trips serious shooters frequently take along clay targets and hand trap for practice shooting or for filling out the day's activities when game is scarce. *By Erwin A. Bauer.*

Used in thick cover, clay targets can sharpen shooter's skill for such game as grouse or woodcock. *By Erwin A. Bauer.*

Biggest target shooting event of the year is Grand American Trap Shooting Championships at Vandalia, Ohio, in late summer. Here tractor-drawn wagon hauls families of shooters along mile-long trap line. *By George Laycock.*

Shooting teams from many parts of the world compete in Grand American at Vandalia. *By George Laycock.*

from the famed shooting grounds of the Grand American at Vandalia, decided that the customary hunting seasons were not giving them as much shooting as they would like. Each autumn they went into the fields for pheasants and rabbits and waded out to their duck blinds where they spent as many productive mornings as they could manage. But with the passing of autumn their shooting for the year was largely done until the following fall. Once they began discussing this unfortunate set of facts they worked out a solution that contains some hints for shooters in many parts of the country.

One of the group had recently inherited a seventeen-acre farm. As practically any farmer will assure you, a piece of land this small will not go far in producing a family living. But the newly acquired land met the needs for a place to shoot. The nine men discussed what they would have to spend to set up a shooting club. It was considerably lower than one might have expected. Each of them put twenty-five dollars in the pot.

The major purchase was equipment for a trap range. The trap was arranged on the brow of a little hill that seemed especially suited to the purpose. The elevation put clear sky behind the flying targets. This made them more easily seen than they would have been against a background of foliage. The hill also enabled the shooters to face the field to the northeast which usually keeps the sun out of a shooter's eyes.

There was only one thing they had not anticipated about the location: the slope beyond the trap field created an updraft. This sometimes gave the targets an added erratic flight pattern. "But that wasn't all bad either," said one of the shooters, "because tricky shooting on a trap range helps prepare you for field conditions."

With this Ohio group there was never any question about constructing a fancy clubhouse. Such a building would have been fine. But it would also have shot the cost of the project beyond what the club members could afford. There was no need for anything but some kind of shelter against sun, wind, and showers. They looked around for a building to convert and found it in an abandoned hoghouse.

The hoghouse was duly moved to a selected spot behind the traps. Then one end was completely knocked out to give a full view of the field from inside. The members acquired a pot-bellied stove for chilly days, made some benches, and imported some cast-off chairs from their home kitchens. Then, with justifiable pride, they christened their new club in honor of the shelter's former occupants: they called their club the Hog House Muskets.

Around the country there are many such local shooting groups. You may see one of them in a farm field on any Sunday afternoon's drive. Its members come for practice, sometimes conduct turkey shoots, or use the club grounds for a picnic. But what these shooting clubs provide most of all, as they did for Hog House Muskets, is an opportunity to keep the shooting eye sharp.

One of the Hog House shooters admitted that before they organized their shooting group it was common enough for him to burn a couple of boxes of shells in the duck blind early in the season without much to show for it. "But now," he added, "a miss on a duck or pheasant is an exception more than the rule."

Another member developed into a good enough shot to come away from the big shoot at Vandalia as high man in his class. All of the members credit their improved shooting ability to the formation of their little club and the regular practice sessions that followed.

Shooting clubs come in wide variety. Some, like the Hog House Muskets, are small and modest. Others may have fancy clubhouses where hundreds of people come to shoot during the year. In addition to skeet and trap, a club can offer such clay target shooting games as a quail walk, duck tower, or rabbit run—all designed to sharpen a shooter's abilities toward the approaching hunting seasons as well as provide sporty shooting in their own right.

Shooters interested in club membership should first investigate the existing clubs in their areas. Some well-equipped clubs with fairly large memberships have annual dues as low as five dollars. Most such clubs, however, depend on the sale of supplies and ammunition to keep them going. In the smaller private clubs the costs are usually split among members.

Those who have been through the process of organizing shooting clubs know the potential pitfalls. Anyone thinking of setting up a shooting club should consider as many aspects of the project in advance as possible. The first step should be to write to the National Shooting Sports Foundation, Inc., 1075 Post Road, Riverside,

Traps can be set to throw birds at variety of angles for practice shooting under various conditions. *By George Laycock.*

Conn. 06878, for a copy of the booklet, *How You and Your Friends Can Start a Gun Club.* The price is fifty cents.

Always a major question is land. The best arrangement is for the club to own its land. Otherwise, after time and money have gone into improvements, the club may find itself dispossessed.

There is always the question about incorporation, insurance, and the costs of starting such a club. These are not overwhelming problems.

What shooters have found in many parts of the country is that organizing their own shooting club—whether fancy or plain—is both easier and less costly than it at first appears. And once established, the shooting club can provide year-round sport at clay target shooting.

Grand American

Gun clubs, and even family groups of shooters, conduct trap shoots and practice sessions, scheduled and unscheduled, in uncounted totals across the country throughout the year. But the biggest of all trap shoots comes in August when shotgunners assemble by the thousands in the otherwise quiet little city of Vandalia, Ohio. They come from practically every state as well as most Canadian provinces and many countries in the world. The attraction is the annual Grand American Trap Shooting Championships, climaxed by the Grand American Handicap. The affair is sponsored by the Amateur Trapshooting Association, P.O. Box 246, Vandalia, Ohio 45377. The membership of this group has been

This trap for throwing clay targets is so low in price that a family of shooters can afford to own one. It is capable of throwing singles or doubles at a variety of angles or elevations. It can be anchored to the ground or mounted on top of an oil drum. *By George Laycock.*

growing rapidly in recent times and is approaching a total of fifty thousand shooters.

The Grand American Tournament, which comprises the Championships and the Handicaps, has been held annually since 1900. Vandalia became its permanent home in 1924. Today the line of traps behind which the shotgunners stand stretches for a mile across the flat Ohio countryside. The shooters bring their families and fill the nearby motels, as well as the campground which springs up on the grounds every year. And if they are lucky, they may take home part of the winnings, because there is big money involved in this shooting event.

In one recent year, the Association logged in 4342 shooters who fired upon nearly two and a quarter million clay targets. The closely cropped green grass in front of the trap line is peppered each year with more than ninety tons of falling shot, according to calculations of Association officials. This turns the trap range into such a lead mine that once every three years the topsoil is processed to reclaim some 250 tons of lead which is sold on the market.

The high point of interest in the week's shooting comes with the Grand American Handicap, where the big money usually goes to some little-known shooter who has a spectacular day. One such shooter in a recent year was Herman Welch, who had come from his home in Illinois for the event. Welch, in spite of the fact that he had been shooting clay targets for several years, had never before won any sizable money and never expected to put his name on the record of winners when he headed for Vandalia.

But after the big day's shooting was finished, Welch said, "When I lifted that gun to my shoulder it felt good. It swung well. After the first few targets I knew I could do it."

What Welch had done was break one hundred targets out of one hundred from his handicap distance of 20½ yards. "Last season," he said incredulously, "I became so disgusted with my shooting I nearly gave up trap shooting. But for some unknown reason I stayed with it." On the day of his victory in Vandalia he was happy about that decision because his purse totaled seven thousand dollars plus a set of sterling silver.

In the history of the Grand no shooter has ever won the big event more than once.

Versatile Trius trap is also capable of throwing tin can targets. *By George Laycock.*

Chapter 13

SKEET SHOOTING

In the early 1920s William H. Foster, assistant editor of *National Sportsman* magazine, began telling his readers about a new shooting game he and some of his friends had devised in their home town of Andover, Massachusetts. Foster called it shooting "around the clock."

The two shooters who had worked out the rules for the game with Foster were C. E. Davies, who operated the Glen Rock Kennels in Andover, and his son Henry Davies. These three shooters hunted birds during the open seasons. The rest of the year, they practiced often on clay targets. The games were fun and the practice kept them sharp.

Then one day they decided to draw a circle and shoot from various stations around it. The circle had a twenty-five-yard diameter. To the shooters it took on the form of a large clock. They marked shooting stations at each of twelve points on the face of the clock.

Next, they installed a trap to throw the clay targets from the twelve-o'clock position so they would rise out over the circle and cross the six-o'clock point. By shooting two shells from each station they obtained from this layout a whole series of angles and a good opportunity for a wide variety of practice shots. The game also guaranteed each shooter an equal chance in competition.

The box of twenty-five shells had one left over, so the inventors of the game decided to shoot the odd shell from the center of the circle at an incoming target. This proved to be such a challenge that it remained in the game. Eventually this extra shot was to be the "optional" shot, and the shooter takes it at his first miss in a round.

The whole idea was working well. Spectators stayed out of the way by following the shooters around the circle. The boy who pulled the trap release used a long cord.

The next important change in the plan, however, owed its origin to chickens. The farmer who owned the land adjacent to the shooting range decided to raise chickens and placed his domestic birds beside the shooting range. This posed some practical problems, the biggest one of which was the spattering of the flock and their keeper with occasional heavy applications of lead shot. The chicken farmer appealed to the shotgunners to adjust their procedure.

In the interest of safety and neighborliness, Foster and the two Davies stood to one side wondering how they might alter their unique shooting range without destroying their original idea. The solution was simple: cut the circle in half. This meant that their guns would be pointing away from the hens.

Then, to provide themselves the same variety of shooting angles, they installed a second trap across the half-circle from the first one. Eventually some of the neighbors came around to join in the shooting games. Other changes were made in the plan as the need for them was discovered. One of the traphouses became a high house. This provided shots at targets following a flatter path instead of having all the shots at rising targets.

With the game now several years old and attracting interest wherever people found out about it, Foster decided it could become a national shooting sport. But it was still called shooting "around the clock." So in February 1926, Foster announced in *National Sportsman* that the search was on for a name for the new game. The prize was one hundred dollars.

From all parts of the country the magazine received a deluge of letters—more than ten thousand of them. One came from Mrs. Gertrude Hurlbutt of Dayton, Montana, who suggested "skeet," probably from the Scandinavian root of "shoot." The suggestion brought her one hundred dollars.

So many people took up the sport that by 1935 the world was ready for the first national skeet championship. In August of that year skeet shooters assembled to compete in Cleveland, Ohio, under the auspices of the recently formed National Skeet Shooting Association. Competitions ceased with World War II, and the Association faded from existence. After the war, however, skeet shooters reformed their defunct organization and in 1946 started out with a national championship shoot in Indianapolis. The money needed to set the new organization in motion came as a loan, without interest, from

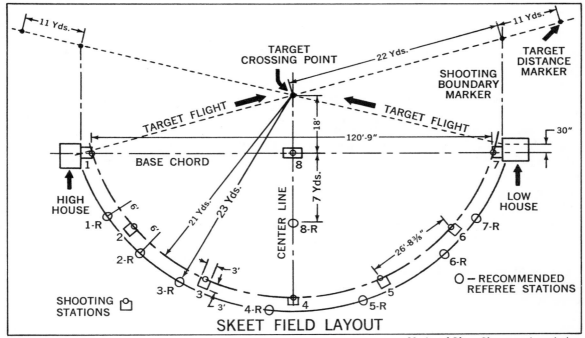

SKEET FIELD LAYOUT

National Skeet Shooters Association

the National Rifle Association.

The 1949 championships were held in Dallas, Texas, with the idea in mind that Dallas would become the permanent home of the Association and the annual big shoot. After four years of journeying to Dallas, however, some of the shooters decided they would like to spend their vacations in other parts of the country. The championships began moving again to various cities. The headquarters of the National Skeet Shooting Association is still in Dallas.

Gradually the shooting game, which started on the kennel club grounds in Andover, Massachusetts, spread beyond the boundaries of the United States to become a worldwide sport. In 1952 skeet, now adopted by the International Shooting Union, was on the program in Oslo, Norway. Today there are skeet shoots held in communities in many parts of the country. The annual world championships draw several hundred shooters.

A round of skeet still consists of twenty-five shots. Two targets are shot from each of the eight stations. One target comes from the low house, an elevation of 3½ feet, and the other from the high house, which is ten feet above ground level. Doubles are shot from stations 1, 2, 6, and 7. The twenty-fifth or "optional" shot provides an-

other chance at the first target missed. And if the shooter breaks all twenty-four targets he can call for his optional shot from his choice of positions.

A skeet squad is composed of five shooters.

The National Skeet Shooting Association recommends the use of standard, commercially made ammunition for registered skeet shoots. The Association, however, does accept the scores of shoots in which reloads have been used, providing the shooter using reloads in a registered shoot indicates to the officials in advance the kind of ammunition he will use, and where the clubs in shoots have approved the use of reloads.

During registered skeet shoots the officials in charge may spot-check the ammunition being used by shooters firing reloaded ammunition. Skeet shooters using their own reloads can be guided by the following official table for allowable maximum shot loads for various gauges.

Gauge	Ounce Load	Grains Standard	Grains Maximum
12	1⅛	492.2	507
20	⅞	382.8	394
28	¾	328.1	338
.410	½	218.8	229

SKEET GUNS

One of the interesting facts about skeet competition is that the shooter is free to use any gun he chooses whether a 12-, 20-, or 28-gauge, or the .410. There are competitions for each gauge. This wide choice of guns allows the shooter to use his field gun for the clay target competition if he chooses. This is especially valuable for the shooter who relies on skeet primarily to keep his shooting eye in condition as preparation for hunting. But the chances are that the skeet shooter who becomes genuinely interested in the competitive phase of the sport, as he is likely to do if he shoots skeet often, will want one or more guns especially for skeet competition.

In recent years gun manufacturers have developed shotguns especially for use on skeet ranges. This does not mean that other guns will not do. In fact, any good field gun, other than a single-shot, will serve well on the skeet range. But the shooter determined to win in major competition begins to look for special skeet models available in the gun shops.

The major thing to remember in selection of a skeet gun is that it must be one that can fire two shots relatively fast, to take care of those doubles. There is no time for loading a fresh shell into a single-shot to get this second bird.

On the skeet range, you may see double-barrel guns, side-by-side, or over-and-under. But there are likely to be more pump guns and autoloaders. Most popular of all among skeet shooters are the autoloaders. With these models the shooter can fire as fast as he is capable of releasing and pulling the trigger.

Skeet guns should have short barrels; because fast handling is important. Most skeet guns have twenty-six-inch barrels. Doubles may have twenty-eight-inch barrels.

Skeet, a shotgun game in which targets are thrown from both high and low houses, was invented to give shooters practice on all kinds of field shots. This skeet range is on an Illinois shooting preserve. *By Erwin A. Bauer.*

Generally, skeet targets are broken at fairly close distances. "Skeet choke" is designed to give a thirty-inch pattern at twenty-five yards.

Most skeet shooters want their shotguns equipped with a ventilated rib, especially if they are using a side-by-side double barrel.

In discussing gauge specifications, the official rules of the National Skeet Shooting Association explain that "Twelve gauge events shall be open to all guns of 12-gauge or smaller, using shot loads not exceeding one and one-eighth (1⅛) ounces. Twenty-gauge events shall be open to all guns of 20-gauge or smaller, using shot loads not exceeding seven-eighths (⅞) of an ounce. Twenty-eight-gauge events shall be open to all guns of 28-gauge or smaller, using shot loads not exceeding three-quarters (¾) of an ounce. Four-ten-gauge events shall be open to .410-gauge guns using shot loads not exceeding one-half (½) ounce. A gun of larger gauge, which has been converted to take a smaller gauge shell may be used in an event for which it has been converted providing that the shell itself complies with the rules requirements for that event. No shot smaller than No. 9 shall be used in any load."

On the skeet range there is a shooting position marked for each station, and one of the shooter's feet must be touching this position when he shoots. His shooting position is a matter of choice, but good shooting form becomes important, especially on the doubles, where there is limited time for the swing and shooting.

The shooter calls "pull," and according to the rules the bird must come from the trap house within one second after he calls. The clay birds follow the same prescribed paths from each trap house, and their paths cross at a point eighteen yards in front of station 8, which is in the middle of the shooting range.

Whether or not you can get into skeet shooting easily will depend largely on whether or not there is a skeet club already organized in your area. There are still large parts of the country without skeet ranges. An active gun club, however, can plan and build such a shooting range with a reasonable investment. And in most parts of the country it will provide year-round shooting.

How much land is needed for a skeet range? The area should be at least six hundred yards by three hundred yards.

SKEET SHOOTING TIPS

Skeet is a game devised to sharpen the shooter's ability to lead and hit flying targets, and as the shooter practices, he picks up skill in knowing how much to lead and when to fire. But for a beginning, the inexperienced shooter can get some idea of the required lead at various stations on a skeet range from the following table.

Station	High House	Low House
1	½ ft. under	1 ft. ahead
2	1½ ft. ahead	1½ ft. ahead
3	3 ft. ahead	3½ ft. ahead
4	3 ft. ahead	3 ft. ahead
5	3½ ft. ahead	3 ft. ahead
6	1½ ft. ahead	1½ ft. ahead
7	1 ft. ahead	Point-blank left side
8	Cover	Cover

Skeet champions insist that the most important single rule in determining how well—or how poorly—a shooter scores is his stance. From each station the shooter should face the point where the birds from the high and low houses will cross courses. Right-hand shooters should have the left foot forward and the toe pointing at the spot where they expect to break the target, which for most shooters is near the crossover point. The left leg should support most of the body weight. This will help bring the body forward into good shooting position. The gun should be pointed somewhat out in front of the trap house; the exact place is something each shooter must learn for himself because it is related to the effectiveness of his eyes and his reflexes in following the targets.

A major safety rule is to bear in mind that shooters never load their guns or close the action until they move into shooting position. Only the person actually shooting ever has a shell in his gun.

Chapter 14

CRAZY QUAIL

One of the latest and most promising variations of the clay bird shooting games is believed to have been a Texas creation. The inventor was seeking a practice method with more built-in challenge than shooters find in the usual clay target games. He dug a pit, walled it, and equipped it with a trap for throwing standard clay targets. The trap was mounted on a revolving arm secured in the pit's concrete floor. The operator rode a comfortable seat on this little merry-go-round so the trap was kept always in front of him.

The pit was deep enough to give the operator complete protection and hide him from view.

Rules for the game called for swinging the trap around and firing the targets in any direction the operator decided to aim—including over the head of the shooter. Anywhere within the 360-degree circle was fair game. What's more, there was no way the shooter could predict when the target would come hurtling out of the hole in the ground. The operator was permitted to hesi-tate as long as he chose after the shooter called "pull."

The shooter must not move his feet once he has called for the clay target. And targets sent back over his station are to be shot before they pass him.

Instead of changing stations, the shooter stands in one spot behind the trap, at a minimum distance of twenty-two yards. By increasing the yardage, shooters can be handicapped.

Here was a shooting game that introduced a new degree of challenge to target practice—the closest thing yet to actually shooting at wild flying birds.

The game was named "crazy quail," and it spread rapidly across the country. It has become especially popular on shooting preserves, where it provides a good opportunity for shooters to brush up on their marksmanship before going into the field for pheasants or quail. If the allotted number of birds is bagged before the hunter gets enough shooting, he can finish off the day with a few rounds on the crazy quail range.

This shooting game can be a good one for a gun club to install. There should be a safe clearance of at least two hundred yards in all directions from the trap pit location. One company, Richmond Sports Products, Inc. of Richmond, Illinois, sells the trap and base in a complete unit for a price within reach of most gun clubs.

State and Federal lands offer hunting opportunities for game such as these big trophy Canada geese. *By George Laycock.*

Chapter 15

WHERE TO HUNT

There can be little question that the lands available for hunting have been diminishing, especially in the heavily populated eastern sections of the United States. The bulldozers and concrete mixers grind on, converting the native land to well-paved wastelands as far as the natural world is concerned. The spreading cities still spread. And the heavily used farmlands seem sometimes to be posted all along the road until the man with the shotgun and hound dog wonders where he might turn for a day in the field. The truth is that the picture, while dark in some neighborhoods, may be less black than it seems.

Even the farmlands posted against hunting are often posted only against those hunters who fail to ask permission. According to one study in a heavily farmed section of Ohio, asking often opens the posted farm gate.

There are state-owned public hunting areas in many states, especially in the eastern half of the country, where they are most needed.

Then there are the national forests. Depending on the part of the country, the forest lands may offer various kinds of game for the hunter, from elk and deer to squirrels and turkeys. The first national forest was the Shoshone, created in Wyoming in 1891. Since that time others have been added until there are now 148, covering more than 181 million acres in thirty-eight states. Aside from the Great Plains states, there are national forest lands in most sections of the country. Not all land within the forest boundaries has yet been bought by the federal government, however.

Hunting is generally free on national forest lands except where the Forest Service has agreements on managed hunts with a few states. Laws governing hunting on national forest lands are set by the game and fish management agencies of the various states.

For additional information about hunting opportunities within the national forests, write either to your state game and fish department or to the nearest regional office of the National Forest Service.

Another agency of the federal government, the Bureau of Land Management, part of the Department of the Interior, manages nearly five times as much acreage as does the National Forest Service in eleven western states. Much of the BLM land is used for grazing, and some is cut off by the gates of private ranchers who, in effect, keep the public off these public lands. The BLM attempts to open such lands as pressure for more recreational use grows. Lands under BLM jurisdiction, like those of the Forest Service, are hunted under the state regulations.

In recent times timber companies have made it plain that visitors are welcome to great sections of their holdings for many kinds of outdoor recreation, hunting included. About fifty-seven thousand companies own American timberlands. Most such companies that permit hunting do so with a system of permits, which helps control the density of hunters at any given time.

Chapter 16

SHOOTING PRESERVES

There was a time when all a hunter had to do to find game was step outside his cabin and look around. As wild game diminished and people increased, hunters traveled farther and farther for their sport or greatly curtailed their hunting.

This was the situation that some years ago led to the creation of shooting preserves where game birds are released for those willing to pay to hunt them. Such shooting preserves provide added hunting opportunities for gunners in most states. According to the National Shooting Sports Foundation, Inc., "All states now have preserve laws enabling preserves to operate." Across the country there are said to be some eight hundred shooting preserves open to the public. Many others are private areas where a group of friends release pheasants in season for their own hunting. In all, there are probably twenty-five hundred or more shooting preserves.

Recently, according to Edward L. Kozicky and John Madson of Olin Industries, there were shooting preserves in forty-eight states harvesting more than two million game birds annually. Kozicky and Madson have played big roles in the development of the shooting preserve idea. As director and assistant director of conservation for the Winchester-Western Division of Olin, they have supervised operation of the famed Nilo Farms near Brighton, Illinois. This seven-hundred-acre farm, some forty miles from St. Louis, became a shooting preserve in 1952. The idea behind its development was to operate Nilo as a demonstration shooting preserve. Soon the growing list of visitors included state game officials. They realized that such areas would play increasingly important roles in the preservation of shooting sports in America. Consequently, Nilo farms helped to speed the acceptance of the preserve idea in numerous states.

To the average gunner this can mean a few extra days of shooting each year, and more if he can afford it. For some living in heavily populated regions the rise of shooting preserves spells the difference between giving up shooting in autumn or keeping their shotguns in use.

The first problem may be locating a nearby shooting preserve. Many do little or no advertising. Local newspaper outdoor writers usually know where the good ones are, however. State game and fish departments often provide such information. The county game protector is a source of information on local shooting preserves.

A shooting preserve may operate on one of three basic plans. Some are private clubs not open to the public. Others are areas where a group of hunters release their birds, do their own work, and split the costs. This plan often involves ten or twelve hunters, including a farmer. The farmer may furnish the land while other members provide the pheasants. The cost of holding pens is shared.

But the third kind, the commercially operated preserve, are the ones with the open gates. The general public is welcome to come and shoot for a set rate per day or bird. The cost of shooting on such an area varies. The average is probably $5 to $6 per pheasant bagged, $2 to $3 per bobwhite, $3.50 to $4.50 for each chukar partridge taken, and $4 to $5 for a mallard.

This may sound high. But chances are that

This pheasant hunter and his dog hunt on private land with owner's permission. *By George Laycock.*

Public hunting areas operated by state conservation agencies provide hunting opportunities for outdoorsmen in many sections of the country. Pheasants are the game most commonly stocked in such areas. *By George Laycock.*

Covey of bobwhite quail rise before a shotgunner on a privately operated shooting preserve in Georgia. *By George Laycock.*

shooting a wild bird could cost a hunter as much. On the shooting preserves the basic difference, aside from the fact that the birds are released, is the fact that the hunter gets more shooting opportunities. The preserve operator is in business to provide shooting. If he does his job well, the paying visitor has plenty of opportunities to shoot.

The most popular of all shooting preserve birds is the ringneck pheasant. He is big and colorful. And besides, he is perpetually wild. Caging a chicken tames him, but the pheasant, even after countless generations of pen-dwelling ancestors, is usually as wild as the wind when turned out. He slips along the brushy fencerow with his long tail low and his head down. If he takes to the wing, he hits the panic button with a force that never fails to challenge a shooter's nerves.

What's more, pheasants are relatively easy to raise in captivity. Some preserve operators raise their own. Others purchase adult birds from commercial pheasant producers. Most have holding pens where the birds are housed and fed until they are released into the fields.

The bobwhite, on the other hand, tends to grow tame in pens and cages. Some preserves, however, keep quail relatively wild with secluded pens which are large enough for the quail to fly in and which contain brush piles in which the birds can hide.

The number of shooting preserves offering mallards are widely scattered. In spite of the fact that old-time duck hunters sometimes degrade preserve shooting as "sliding them in on a wire," this brand of controlled duck shooting can be anything but easy. On some preserves gunners may average a dozen 12-gauge shells expended for each mallard taken.

The ducks usually fly from a tower on a hill over the treetops to a pond four hundred yards or more away. Blinds are hidden in the woods along the flight path, where the ducks may speed downhill at sixty miles an hour.

One of the more successful shooting preserves in the country is the Cherry Bend Pheasant Farm near Wilmington, Ohio. A look at its operation will give shooters an insight into what they might encounter in a day's shooting on such a preserve. Cherry Bend, which produces and releases more than fifteen thousand pheasants a year, covers 368 acres of highly productive grain farming land. It is within easy driving distance of Cincinnati, Dayton, Columbus, and various smaller cities.

The preserve shooting season here lasts eight months. Hunters usually call in advance for reservations. They pay twenty dollars a day, and this entitles them to three pheasants, two cock birds, or three hens. They can shoot as many more as they want at an additional charge. After the hunt they can, for a small charge, have their birds dressed and wrapped, ready for the freezer. Each game farm bird has a shipping tag attached to one leg so it can be legally transported when the season on wild pheasants is closed.

During the hunting season Cherry Bend releases pheasants every day, and often several times a day. The fields are planted with thick-growing sorghum and grass crops to provide cover for the birds.

Here a dog is almost an essential. But the hunter who does not own a bird dog can come anyway. Cherry Bend supplies trained and experienced dogs as companions at no added cost.

Some shooting preserves maintain kennels and a supply of dogs for their guests. One such operation is the Cherry Bend Pheasant Farm, Wilmington, Ohio, shown here. *By George Laycock.*

Pheasant hunter gets a fast shot at a shooting-preserve cock pheasant. Shooting-preserve seasons last several months and provide hunting at times when public hunting seasons are closed elsewhere. *By George Laycock.*

Most shooting preserves do not furnish dogs, especially without sending their own guide along.

Cherry Bend also has an airstrip on one end of the farm for the convenience of flying sportsmen. They release only pheasants. Some other preserves release more than one kind of bird.

There is a trend today toward turning shooting preserves into complete year-round family outdoor recreation areas. Some offer swimming, fishing, archery ranges, riding stables, and campgrounds.

Many shooting preserves have installed crazy quail installations where shooters can sharpen up on clay targets. One recent survey reveals that more than half of the preserves in business offer some form of clay target shooting.

At Henderson, Colorado, Ann and Dave Howe have even established highly popular shooting classes and dog training classes on their Gunner's Mark Preserve. At Goose Lake, Iowa, John Mullin offers conservation tours of his Arrowhead Preserve for students and also gives shooting instruction.

If you are rusty on your shooting—or even a rank beginner—the well-operated shooting preserve will provide you with a place to sharpen up. Some preserve operators suggest that visiting shooters—if they have never been on the area previously—first work out on the clay targets. Many provide guides who are glad to coach the shooter requesting help. This is one of the reasons why the shooting preserve is a good place to introduce young hunters to field sports.

The chances are good that the shooting preserve idea will become increasingly important to hunters living in highly populated areas. If preserve operators insist on releasing strong-flying, well-feathered birds under conditions as natural as they can make them, the hunter will welcome the added opportunity to shoot—even if he misses.

Chapter 17

RABBITS

Rabbits, it seems, are everywhere, or nearly so—and hunting them is a time-honored American tradition. This is the hunting on which farmboys begin. And having savored it in their youth, they never completely outgrow the adventure and excitement that comes with chasing cottontails through the fields.

There are, in various parts of the country, several kinds of rabbits and hares. There are marsh rabbits, swamp rabbits, jackrabbits, and big snowshoe hares. But far and away, the rabbit that attracts the greatest attention is the common cottontail. These dashing little natives have adapted so readily to human surroundings that they are common around our yards in both city and country.

The cottontail must make a perpetual effort to save his hide. Working in his favor are his brown coat, his dashing speed, and his elusiveness—all of which enliven the hunt.

Rabbits are vegetarians. They thrive on grass, weeds, and the buds and tips of shrubs. Sometimes they will, when faced by food shortages, turn to bark of fruit trees and girdle them. They are usually found around thick-growing vegetative cover. Briar patches are classic home territories for cottontails. So are weedy ditches and brushy fencerows. Never overlook such hiding places as culverts, old rolls of fencing, and brush piles.

On bright warm days a rabbit may be out in the tall grass, crouched down among the roots resting. If there is a high wind look on the lee of the slopes. In rainy weather, or bitterly cold days, rabbits may seek security in some hole in the ground or brush pile from which it is extremely difficult to rout them. Even when out in open fields, the cottontail is seldom far from heavy protective cover.

After a snowfall, providing the weather is not too cold, is often a good time to go rabbit hunting. A light snow not only does not bother them, but also makes it possible to find their tracks.

But if there has been a deep snow the chances of finding many rabbits out running are slight.

It is possible to hunt rabbits with no help from man or dog, but such solo work is much less productive than taking along a couple of beagles or bassets. And it is less fun. Beagles have been developed over the decades for just this type of hunting. They have the nose for tracking. And they are persistent. Nothing in the world interferes with his tracking if a beagle can help it. A good beagle loves to hunt, and is always ready to go. Besides, the beagle is a first-rate family dog.

Among the most popular species of American game are the rabbits. This hunter gets added elevation by perching on a stump during a hunt for swamp rabbits in western Kentucky. *By George Laycock.*

A hard-working beagle makes an excellent companion for a rabbit hunter and provides him with shots he would otherwise never get. *By Erwin A. Bauer.*

The cottontail is a swift-footed, darting target—a test of the shotgunner's skill. *By Erwin A. Bauer.*

In addition, the good rabbit dog is slow. Running rabbits follow a pattern. They have home territories which they are reluctant to leave. They sometimes have favorite trails to which they return. So the rabbit hunter stands his best chance by waiting for the rabbit to make a round trip back to the place where the dog jumped him in the first place. Stand and listen to the slow-poke dog sing, and sooner or later he brings the rabbit doubling back to you.

Larger species of rabbits may follow larger circles. A snowshoe hare may take considerable time to come back around, and cover a mile or two in the process. He is a large, strong creature

and fully capable of pushing through swamps and evergreens for several hours at a time.

Swamp rabbits, somewhat bigger than their cottontail cousins, also tend to travel in larger circles. But the thing to remember is that playing the waiting game usually pays off.

Among the hardest-working beagles I ever saw was a pack of swamp rabbit specialists owned by my friend, Lee Nelson, a Kentucky outdoorsman who favored hunting these wetland rabbits over ordinary cottontails. Some years ago four of us arrived early one cold winter morning in the flooded timberlands of the Ohio River bottom in western Kentucky. In that thick-growing brush it was impossible to see very far. By climbing up on a log or stump we could increase our field of vision.

Swamp rabbits are quick to take to the water, or elude the hounds by running on top of logs. You may get only one quick glimpse of the patch of fur dashing through an opening in front of you, and if you are quick enough, and accurate enough in your gun handling, you may score. Swamp rabbit hunters earn their game, and a day of this uncommon brand of hunting is one to remember.

Practically any shotgun will be satisfactory, with the possible exception of the .410, which many hunters consider too small for rabbit hunting. A far better choice in normal brushy cover where rabbits live is either the 20-, 16-, or 12-gauge with a modified choke. At the ranges in which rabbits are often running, a full choke, if it scores, is likely to destroy the meat. A repeating gun is desirable. The best all-round shell for the job is a low-brass No. 6. These pattern well, penetrate a moderate amount of brush, and carry enough impact to stop the game. Some hunters, in more open situations, prefer a smaller shot, such as No. 7½, and a full choke. But this combination is not at its best for most cottontail shooting.

Rabbit hunters worry considerably about tularemia. The best precaution against this disease is to carry a good pair of rubber gloves, and wear them every time a rabbit is handled. Usually only a small percentage of rabbits in the wild are diseased. Those that appear sluggish can be left alone. Remember that thorough cooking renders wild rabbits entirely safe to eat. But do not feed the livers and other raw parts to your dog unless you want him to get tularemia.

Rabbits live in the brushy places near openings where they can feed on succulent green vegetation. *By Savage Arms.*

Chapter 18

SQUIRRELS

There was a day in the history of America when squirrel hunting fed families. It is true that today's squirrel hunters seldom pursue their game out of necessity, but the native squirrels still hold their appeal to the woodsman. The meat is still widely favored among outdoorsmen, and the hunting is challenge out of all proportion to the size of the game.

Good squirrel hunters are good woodsmen. The squirrels are so alert and elusive that taking them consistently calls forth talents in stalking, patience, and the reading of the natural signs that might reveal the presence of game. The hunter expecting to go into the deer woods with the opening of the fall season can do no better than practice his woodsmanship on squirrels. Many of the techniques of slipping up on wild game work equally well on deer or squirrels.

Most of the squirrel hunting done in this country is practiced on gray or fox squirrels. The gray squirrel is the most widely distributed. The black squirrel found in some northern states is a color phase of the gray squirrel. The gray squirrels are usually found in the more heavily wooded regions, the hardwood forests that provide them shelter from predators as well as an abundance of such foods as acorns, hickory nuts, and beechnuts. They are not above taking corn from the edges of the farmer's fields where the corn borders the woodlands. Often, especially in a poor nut year, the quiet hunter can hear squirrels rattling corn stalks as they attempt to husk the grain for their own harvest. There is less known about the food habits of the western gray squirrel which inhabits the pine and oak woodlands of the Pacific Coast.

The fox squirrel, which weighs about twice as much as the gray species, is found throughout the eastern part of the country, although elimination of woodlots has made it a rarity in some communities. This big squirrel is often found more in the open woodlots than is the gray squirrel. A fox squirrel living in the open woodlands or along the edge of the forest where open fields are handy usually has a favorite den tree. But he may roam considerable distances for food. If you intercept him in these travels, given half a chance he heads for home at a speed which carries him over the ground at about eleven miles an hour.

More than the gray squirrel, the fox squirrel is likely to be out at midday, feasting or perhaps resting on a limb or a platform of leaves.

The hunter who would bag a meal of gray squirrels, however, gets out early. By the first rays of daylight he is in the woods, because gray squirrels get up early. The gray squirrel is a litterbug, a fact which often gives away his location. You can tell when he is feeding because of the rattling leaves or the sound of shells and bits of twigs falling. He will also be out feeding again in the evening unless the weather is too rainy or blustery.

There are at least four good plans for hunting squirrels. The simplest of all is for the hunter to find a good food tree beneath which fresh cuttings litter the earth. Take a seat beneath the

Squirrel hunting is often a sitting game. Well aware of this, some hunters take camp stools into the squirrel woods with them. *By George Laycock.*

Squirrel hunters can frequently pick out good areas by checking for tracks left by squirrels that glean their meals from the edges of corn fields. *By George Laycock.*

tree, preferably where you can also see into surrounding trees, and wait. The hunter who waits quietly enough on such a stand may take not one but several squirrels from the same tree.

Squirrels can also be stalked. Move through the woodlands slowly. Stop often for several minutes at a time. Watch and listen. If you spot a squirrel out of range, attempt to move into range during those moments when his attention is elsewhere or when there is a tree between you.

One variation of this kind of hunting is to use a dog. Good squirrel dogs are often small mongrels that delight in treeing squirrels.

Or you can try floating for squirrels. Drift down a woodland stream in a canoe or johnboat and study the foliage for signs of squirrels feeding or traveling. If the hunting is slow, there is the possibility of laying the gun aside and catching a smallmouth bass or a catfish for the skillet.

Squirrels have a habit of putting a protective tree between themselves and the hunter. Some-

times a stick or stone thrown into the brush on the other side of the tree will accomplish the desired result. Some hunters working alone have even fooled squirrels by tying a long string to a bush on the far side of the nut tree. When the squirrel is working out of sight, the string is jerked. The startled squirrel just may come darting around the tree and into range.

Some squirrel hunters insist that the only sporting way of taking these animals is with a small-caliber rifle. But the fact remains that a great majority of the squirrels bagged are taken with shotguns. It is a matter of choice. One handy compromise is the combination shotgun and rifle, such as the Savage Model 24, which combines the .22 with either the .410 or 20-gauge.

Within range, the choice of gauge in a squirrel gun makes less difference than the size of the shot. The squirrel is tougher than might be suspected, and a fairly sizable shot size—No. 6 is a good choice—is in order.

Chapter 19

PHEASANTS

The pheasant is always popular. His colors shame the rainbow, and once reduced to possession roast pheasant becomes a delicacy on the family table.

In addition, the pheasant on the wing—while not the world's most elusive target—provides as much challenge as an average shotgunner can handle. A heavy old cock pheasant rocketing from the weed patch, cheering himself on to full effort with his own cackling, can momentarily shake the confidence of a hunter. More often than many outdoorsmen like to admit, the bird goes hurtling off toward some distant thicket or weed patch untouched.

Sophisticated hunters sometimes discredit the pheasant as a game bird, claiming that shooting them is too easy for anyone even slightly acquainted with the handling of a shotgun. In most circles this snobbish approach will be recognized for what it is. No one can make generalizations about the ease with which a pheasant can be shot. The reason lies in the fact that no one can predict, with certainty, what the flushed pheasant will do. Some do exactly what you would have them do, flush where you anticipate, fly in the direction you expect, climb at an angle you predict, and fall where they are quickly found. This total situation is often far removed from the actual case.

It is true that if you should suspend a pheasant from a string at thirty-five yards it is a simple matter to hit him with a pattern of shot. But most pheasants do not stand still in midair at the accepted range. Instead they may be practicing any number of deceptive flight tactics. Watch a pheasant in a strong wind climb skyward like a mallard duck, then lose elevation instead of gaining it, slip air off one wing, crab into the wind, hurtle along at weedtop level, or come abruptly to earth and take up his running game again. The gunner will find enough surprises in pheasant hunting to keep his senses alert.

Why are pheasants missed? Often it is because the gun is pointed where they are instead of where they are going to be. In the instant that follows two things happen. The trigger is pulled and pheasant has forged ahead on his air lane. The pheasant's long tail sometimes fools the hunter. Many a bird has lost nothing but his tail feathers and his dignity in what the hunter would have sworn was going to be a head shot.

The angle at which the bird is rising can fool a hunter. When a bird is gaining altitude, it is an easy matter to shoot beneath him. Let the pheasant get out of the proper range for the gun and the load you are using. There is a moment in the going-away flight of a pheasant that is just right for the shot.

As for the choice of shotguns, the 12-gauge is the most popular. Most experienced pheasant hunters consider a modified choke best. The gun should be one that is easily carried and smoothly handled in the field. Pump guns and autoloaders are popular for pheasant hunting because of the speed with which one can get off second and third shots. The pheasant is a big, tough bird and the shots are not always close in. The most common load—and best under most circumstances— is a No. 6 shot. Smaller shot are often too light for the job.

Some pheasant hunters use 20-gauges, and a few even try bagging these birds with .410s. The 20 may do the job, but the .410 is out of its class in the pheasant fields.

Pheasants are birds of the farmlands, especially the fertile fields of the Midwest and the rich, irrigated valleys of western states. There is pheasant hunting available on some public hunting areas maintained by state game and fish agencies, on a few national wildlife refuges in season, and on privately operated shooting preserves. But a large part of the pheasant hunting is still practiced on the farmer's land.

In some of the best pheasant shooting areas farm owners have organized into associations that set fees for hunting within townships or other political subdivisions. The better pheasant hunting states—Nebraska and the Dakotas—cash in on this natural resource by advertising heavily for out-of-state hunters.

There are several methods of hunting pheasants, but the success of any of them is likely to hinge on understanding the bird, how he lives, how he moves from area to area, and especially how he reacts to the pressure of continued hunting by men and dogs. A good dog is almost an

For many shotgunners the king of the game birds is the big, noisy, gaudy, ring-neck pheasant, such as this one which rose from the edge of a woodlot before an Ohio gunner and his dog. *By George Laycock.*

These hunters on Pelee Island in Lake Erie display results of their pheasant hunt; in some years the birds are so abundant that hens are included in the bag limit. *By George Laycock.*

essential for serious pheasant hunters. Without the dogs hunters can easily walk past tight-sitting birds they never suspected were there.

The favorite strategy of a pursued pheasant is not to fly, but to run. Given a travel lane of thick-growing cover, he can slip along close to the ground at a speed that keeps him well ahead of the advancing gunner. But the hunter who understands this trait can make use of it, and this is one reason why pheasant hunting is usually more successful for a group than for a single hunter.

One method is to divide the group and station one-half at the end of the corn field or weed patch. The other half drives the field, moving the birds toward the hunters on stand. Then it is turnabout and, in the next field, the drivers become standers. If there are too few people working a field, the birds may slip back between the advancing line or spill out over the edges of the fields before they are moved to the end where the hunters wait.

Those driving the birds get occasional shots at pheasants that take to the air, but most of the shots will ordinarily go to the men on stand.

Obviously, this is the situation where there is much necessity for careful gun handling. Drivers should stay in line, and low-angle shots are to be avoided. Some say that anybody who would shoot a bird on the ground would steal a baby's bottle. The exception is a crippled bird. He should be taken as soon as possible. Here is more work for the dog.

A smart pheasant hunter, accompanied by one smart dog, can put many a bird in the game bag. Look for situations where you can work long cover lanes that empty into brushy areas or pockets of evergreens. These are dead-end streets for pheasants. Work the fencerows and ditches leading to such cover patches. If the area is small, a lone hunter may flush birds within gun range frequently, even without a dog. Work through the area, but stop occasionally for a short period and wait. Maintain a steady pace, and the wise old cock pheasant may crouch and hide right beside your hunting boot without abandoning his position. But the stop-and-go technique disconcerts him. When he can take no more he gets out and travels, sometimes when the hunter has already passed him.

This pheasant was taken on an Illinois shooting preserve. *By Winchester-Western.*

The pheasant rises with the commotion that excites dogs and hunters alike. Hunters should not underestimate the pheasant's ability nor the lead that might be required if they are to bag him. *By Winchester-Western.*

The best time of the year to score well on pheasants is early in the season. Huntable pheasants are at peak populations, and hunters and dogs are eager for the field. The year's crop of young cock birds has not yet been conditioned to hunting. The pheasants at this season are usually spread well over their range and are found in hay fields, corn fields, weed patches, and near the edges of country roads. So far, nothing has driven them to thicker protective cover, and wherever you hunt you may get up a bird. They are not likely at this time to have retired to the woodlots.

Like many kinds of game birds, pheasants do most of their feeding early and late in the day, and then especially they can be found in the open areas where there is grain and weed seed. Between feeding periods they are often resting in thicker cover.

As the season wears on, the elusive pheasants become increasingly difficult to take. In heavily hunted territory an experienced pheasant may develop a bagful of tricks. In fall-plowed fields you may on occasion find one hiding in the shade of a large clod, but chances are you won't spot him until he takes to the air. In such open situations, the tracks in fresh snow sometimes give away the bird's hiding place.

In rainy weather or when there is a stiff wind blowing, the birds are likely to be in areas that offer them protection from the elements. Wind may keep them out of the fields of unpicked corn where the rattling leaves might mask the approach of predators. At such times they are often found in grassy ditches. As the season wears on, and the remaining birds become increasingly wary, do not overlook even the unlikely places. They may be found around old buildings, in the woods, and even around old junk piles. Cattail marshes are good hiding places for ringnecks. In some areas marshes are roosting places that attract pheasants from surrounding fields.

Since they were first imported, pheasants have been tried in practically every part of the country. Aside from venturing north or west for the annual hunting seasons, hunters living beyond pheasant territory can find these birds in dozens of commercial shooting preserves across the country. They are relatively easy to raise in large numbers, but they seldom lose their wildness—which makes them a challenge in the field.

Chapter 20

QUAIL HUNTING

Across the country there are half a dozen kinds of native quail. Five of them are western birds, while one occupies all of the east. The western quail include the harlequin, found on wooded slopes from New Mexico down into Mexico. The mountain quail of western states is a large quail with a long, slender head plume. Two quail, the California and Gambel's, look much alike in their markings, and each wears a topknot that broadens and hangs over at the top. The scaled quail lives in the desert country of the Southwest and Mexico, where it is sometimes found in flocks of several dozen birds. It is a strong runner, a fact which can frustrate both hunter and dogs.

But through the eastern half of the country and in the South, an invitation to go after "birds" means only one thing—the season has arrived for seeking out the bobwhite coveys. Through the southeastern states the bobwhite is king of game birds. When the bird season opens hunters are likely to put everything else aside and take their dogs to the fields where the quail coveys live.

There is a magic moment as the dog slides to a halt and tells his owner by the rigid point where the birds are hidden in front of him. Will the shooter remember the lessons of the past and calmly pick his shots, or will the unpredictable birds get him confused and cause him to waste the

Part of the thrill of quail hunting is watching good dogs at work. This pointer has a covey spotted and holds his rigid point while the hunters move in. *By George Laycock.*

opportunity? Quickly he walks in beside his dogs, and the covey rockets noisily into the air around him. At this time the beginner sometimes makes the mistake of firing into the heart of the covey, without picking his bird. Later he doesn't see how he ever missed them all—but he did.

Often, locating a covey of quail is not difficult. The person who lives in the country knows where the birds are heard and seen in the fields and weed patches. The stranger, however, may have to prospect for them. Where do you look? Avoid the timberlands and the clean-tilled agricultural fields. Search instead the brushy areas, pastures bordered by thick-growing fencerows, small patches of woods or pine thickets with good cover beneath them.

The bobwhite normally feeds in the early morning and again late in the afternoon. His favored foods are weed seeds and grains. To find the coveys in midday, search the thicker cover where the birds rest between feeding periods. They frequently stick tighter in cold, rainy days.

But the birds from a flushed and scattered covey seldom travel out of sight, and the hunter can mark them down. Then he can work them as singles, because the chances are good that his pointer can locate some of them and hold them until they are flushed. One other method sometimes used on the singles is to wait a quarter hour, then use a quail call to locate the birds by their answers.

Biologists have learned that bobwhites suffer tremendous turnovers in their populations each year. Usually 80 percent or more of the bobwhites alive in autumn will be dead by spring whether from predation, disease, starvation, weather, or hunting.

Good sportsmanship, however, calls for leaving the covey before its numbers are seriously depleted. Usually nature takes a firm hand in this. As the size of the covey grows smaller, the remaining birds become wilder and more difficult to find and shoot.

Whatever gun is normally used for hunting other upland game will do for quail. Many quail hunters prefer a small gun with a short barrel. Most shots are at short to medium range, and a modified choke is the best all-round choice. Shot sizes should be small, preferably No. 7½s or No. 8s.

Chapter 21

MOURNING DOVE

In the average year an estimated thirty million mourning doves go home in the pockets of hunter's coats. And it is estimated that every dove bagged requires the firing of four shells.

Whether or not the mourning dove is actually as fast on the wing as he appears when swooping past a shotgunner is sometimes ques-tioned. Although he may fly thirty to forty miles an hour, speed is not the whole story.

One opening day I was hunting in a Kentucky grain field. I still recall vividly the first bird that came into range. I heard the rustling of his wings. He was speeding along the fencerow right toward my back. I swung, saw him, and brought my 16-gauge up all in the same moment.

But as I saw the bird he also spotted me, dropped one wing, raised the other, and altered course by 90 degrees. He went into a steep climb toward the center of the field. The pressure was already on the trigger, and I could not recall the shot. I knew in that instant that I was about to miss the first dove of the day by a country mile. The shot was somewhere beneath and be-

Among the fastest of all birds shotgunners pursue are mourning doves. These were collected on a Kentucky hunt. *By George Laycock.*

hind that dove. It was like throwing dust at a shadow, and not until several doves later did I begin to settle down and score. A dove like that can help a person understand why there are four shells fired for every dove taken home.

Doves are hunted today in about two-thirds of the states. They live, however, in forty-eight states, and could safely be taken in more states than they are as far as the biological security of the species is concerned.

This longtime controversy has prompted wildlife biologists to investigate in detail the mourning dove's life cycle and biotic potential many times

in many places. Doves are probably more abundant today than they were before the settling of the country. Millions of them find suitable nesting cover in the evergreens and decorative shrubs around suburban homes. Farm grains provide them with feed and farm ponds with watering places.

But the life span of the average mourning dove is brief—not because they are hunted, but because by the rules of nature the life expectancy of this bird never has been great. The average mourning dove can look forward to less than a year of life. They replace themselves rapidly.

Hunting doves does not require an elaborate blind. This hunter crouches next to the edge of a sorghum field. *By Erwin A. Bauer.*

Study after study has indicated that up to 70 percent of the doves alive in late summer will be dead by the following spring, whether they are hunted or not.

There are several ways to hunt doves. Methods vary with the number of hunters in the group, weather, whether early or late in the season, and the local farming practices. Doves roost in flocks, often in such places as apple orchards. They fan out to their feeding areas early in the morning. During the middle of the day they may rest, especially if the weather is hot. Then they normally feed again late in the afternoon. Finally, they will fly to their favorite watering holes, then move into their roosting cover.

If they perform all these acts in the anticipated manner they may be intercepted at several places along their daily flight paths. Unfortunately, doves can't always be trusted. They may shift feeding, roosting, and watering areas without notice, especially if hunting pressure is heavy in an area for several days. They may also vary their daily time schedule.

It is a good idea, before opening day, to cruise the countryside and locate their feeding areas. These offer the best opportunities for shooting. Hunters intent on finding doves coming to water or flying into their roosts, hide along the paths they expect the birds to follow.

Some hunters successfully walk doves up from their feeding or resting areas. But ordinarily this is not the most frutiful hunting. Most dove shooters prefer to organize their hunt. A group of shooters stationed around a grain field can usually keep the birds moving.

Decoys are sometimes used successfully. Usually these are plastic or heavy cardboard. Often they are simple silhouettes grouped in the open where the passing birds can see them. Most hunters who use decoys prefer to place them on the limbs of bushes or trees where the outlines stand out boldly against the sky.

If you are prone to try long shots, select a gun with full choke. Some dove shooters prefer to pass up the long shots. They use a modified choke and let the birds come to within thirty-five yards or so. Small shot, No. 7½ or No. 8 will do nicely.

Chapter 22

GROUSE

There may not be a finer native game bird in all of North America than the ruffed grouse. This chunky brownish or grayish woodland bird is shaped somewhat like a banty chicken. It is wary and elusive, a feathered rocket that comes bounding out of the thickets with a speed and noise that shakes up even the level-headed oldtimers.

The excitement of this woodland chicken's explosive takeoff just doesn't wear off for anyone with even a spark of interest in the outdoors.

And hitting a ruffed grouse with a shotgun is challenge enough for almost anyone. In one organized grouse hunt in a southern Ohio public hunting area recently, forty hunters fired seventy-seven rounds and brought back only six birds. That's what the grouse can do.

In some parts of its range this bird is known as partridge or "pat." In the southern Appalachians it is sometimes called "mountain pheasant." Ruffed grouse live in the northern half of the United States from Maine to Oregon, and ornithologists have identified twelve subspecies.

While the type of habitat will vary with local conditions and the native vegetation, ruffed grouse

Along the Continental Divide high up in the Rocky Mountains of Colorado, these hunters pursue the white-tailed ptarmigan. *By George Laycock.*

Any shotgunner who consistently takes the fast-flying, brush-dodging ruffed grouse may count himself among the expert shots. *By George Laycock.*

White-tailed ptarmigan taken along the Continental Divide in September, when birds change from summer to winter plumage. *By George Laycock.*

The sage grouse is an important game bird in many western areas. This shoot occurred in Montana. *By Erwin A. Bauer.*

These three hunters, each carrying a different type of shotgun, including pump gun, automatic, and double-barrel, have had a successful hunt for white-tailed ptarmigan along the Continental Divide in Colorado. *By George Laycock.*

are seldom found far from brushy, thick-growing cover. And they are located in young timber stands more likely to be abandoned farmlands than mature forests. Brushy openings in the forest provide them with food and cover.

The ruffed grouse has a well-known talent for drumming. If you are in the field in April or May you might hear them sending their muffled drumming through the woodlands. The best time of day to hear them is at daylight.

Biologists who census grouse each year follow prescribed routes, usually driving back roads through the forests and stopping at regular intervals to listen. They record the frequency and location of calls. Hunters looking forward to the coming fall's grouse hunt can do the same thing. If everything goes according to schedule, the location of drumming grouse should mark the approximate areas in which broods of young will appear.

How does the grouse make his drumming sound? It is not, as some have suspected, a matter of beating his wings against a hollow log or even against his chest. Instead he beats them only against the air. The drumming begins on a low note, slowly at first, gaining speed until it becomes a roll. It is sounded only by the male

The grouse hunter's prize is a handsome but well-camouflaged bird. *By George Laycock.*

Wisconsin grouse hunter Wilbur Stites lets his German shorthair inspect the bird he just bagged. *By George Laycock.*

from some favorite log within his territory.

The nest, usually at the base of a large tree, is no more than a hollow depression in the leaves. Here, after about twenty-four days, the dozen or so eggs hatch. The chicks are up and running through the woods with their mother as soon as they are dry.

One early November day in the hills of southern Ohio, I worked along the edge of a ridge until I came to a great fallen oak tree. The limbs and leaves provided a magnificent tangled jungle where birds could hide. As I

paused in front of the downfall, a grouse erupted from the far side with a roar of wings that sounded like a woodsman starting up his chainsaw. I didn't even see him. He managed to keep the brush pile neatly between us.

It was too late now to move around to the other side of the downfall. As I contemplated this, two more birds came hurtling from the brush and made off safely to the woodlands. In all there were six grouse secluded in that one big brush pile. Every one of them escaped. In such a situation two hunters with a good dog stand a far better chance of scoring than does a single hunter. Good grouse dogs are uncommon compared with the number of dogs that perform creditably on pheasants. But the value of a grouse dog can hardly be overestimated. He can penetrate cover his owner can only walk around and with the aid of his nose locate birds that would otherwise be missed. But grouse cover is usually thick, and the dog needs to stay in close.

Grouse, like many game birds, are most likely to feed early and late in the day. This, providing you know what they are eating locally, can be a clue to their location. They are frequently found around the wild grape tangles and the greenbrier patches. They are likely to feed on soft fruits early in the fall. Later they may turn to beechnuts, acorns, and buds.

The grouse hunter should dress in hunting coat and trousers designed to protect against briers. Often, by pushing noisily right into a greenbrier patch, a hunter can flush grouse that otherwise stick tight.

On bleak, cold days look for grouse in heavier cover. In such weather they may move into patches of evergreen, and it pays to glance upward occasionally when hunting a stand of evergreen.

Grouse once flushed and missed can often be marked down and followed up for a second try. They frequently fly to other cover similar to that from which they are flushed.

In some areas grouse seasons are the longest of all hunting seasons. In Ohio, for example, the season normally lasts 4½ months, without damage to the population.

The ruffed grouse has some impressive cousins. The spruce grouse lives in the northern evergreens. It is sometimes called "fool hen" because it is foolishly tame where men are concerned. While on pack trips I have often seen these big grouse fly to a low limb of a tree and sit there as horsemen rode beneath them almost close enough to reach out and pick them from their perches. In western mountains the big blue grouse is an excellent game bird. Prairie chickens are also members of the grouse family. The prairie chickens are, as their name implies, inhabitants of the open lands. Their numbers have decreased so much in recent years that only in a few areas are there still enough of them to permit open seasons. The changing environment, not hunting, has been the major cause of the prairie chicken's downfall

in recent times. The sharptail lives somewhat farther north and occupies the brushlands and the clearings in addition to the open prairie country.

Hunters carry a wide variety of shotguns into the grouse woods. This is an excellent place for a 20-gauge. The shots on grouse are often fairly close and the lighter, shorter gun is easier to handle fast in rough cover. Many grouse hunters prefer an autoloader or a pump gun because of the speed with which they can fire second and third shots. Often there is precious little time for the hunter to swing on a grouse and line up the bird before it puts a tree between itself and the gun.

For ruffed grouse, select a smaller shot size. No. 7½ or No. 8 shot are good sizes.

Ruffed grouse follow population cycles which reach a peak about once every ten years. Some states, aware that it is difficult to overhunt these birds, permit grouse hunting over periods of two months or more each fall and winter. *By George Laycock.*

This Ohio grouse hunter brings his bird down successfully before it can dart behind the trees and escape. *By George Laycock.*

This Ohio grouse hunter uses a shotgun with an adjustable choke device. Grouse more than some other game birds are difficult for dogs to work. A good grouse dog can be extremely important for a successful day's hunt. *By George Laycock.*

In parts of the West, the sage grouse is a favorite game bird with the shotgunner. *By George Laycock.*

Chapter 23

WILD TURKEYS

There are few greater thrills in the hunter's experience than calling a wary old turkey gobbler to within thirty or forty yards. The turkey is a majestic, alert, elusive creature whose loud gobbling call can set nerves to tingling. Fortunately, opportunities for taking wild turkeys are increasing, not decreasing, in many parts of the country. There are two major reasons. Timberlands have recovered from destructive timbering practices once followed. And wildlife biologists have learned the techniques of live-trapping and transplanting pure strain wild turkeys which often succeed where game farm birds fail.

One good example of a state that has succeeded in bringing back a breeding population of the all-American bird is Ohio. Recently, when the state held its first open season on wild turkeys in more than sixty years, I spent the opening morning far back in southeastern Ohio's most rugged timbered hill country.

Well ahead of daylight I was settled on a point overlooking a wooded hollow. In the valley below me, Wayne Bailey of West Virginia and C. Eugene Knoder, who reintroduced the ancestors of these turkeys to Ohio, were engaged in plans of their own. Daylight had scarcely cracked the sky when I heard the first gobbler call. It came from somewhere below me.

I waited a respectable interval, then sounded the yelping hen call on the box call I carried. The old bird responded at once, and his gobbling answer rolled up the wooded hillside. I waited, then called once more. But the answering gobble did not come for another five minutes. And when it did the old male had not moved closer, as I fully expected, but farther away. Something about my performance as a hen turkey had failed to titillate him.

There were two gobblers in the immediate area we were hunting, and every morning of the hunt one or more of us made contact with them. I saw them both on two mornings, and once had them come almost within range. But they

spooked and took to the air in a display of magnificent flying, dodged branches and gained altitude, then alternately flapped and glided until lost in the forest perhaps half a mile away. The hunt was over for these birds, at least for the moment.

What can spook a turkey? The answer is anything at all that seems out of place in their woods. Their eyesight is extremely sharp, and their hearing is at least average. A slight motion in the underbrush a hundred yards distant may be all that is needed to send them out of the community.

Experienced turkey hunters know this well. Consequently, no effort to seclude themselves is too great, no trouble in fooling the bird too much to take. Somber-colored clothing that fits into the general color of the woods is in order. Camouflage clothing is all right if it is not hard-finish cloth, which scrapes noisily against branches. When trying to call up a turkey, hide yourself in the brush where you think that old gobbler is going to come out. Have your gun pointed and ready. Often the movement of the

Wisconsin is among those states to which the wild turkey has returned as a huntable species in recent times. This turkey was taken on a hunt in Meadow Valley in 1966. *By Wisconsin Conservation Dept.*

gun muzzle gives a turkey time to duck behind cover.

There is no question about whether or not the bird in your sights is a turkey. The big gobbler may measure four feet in length, stretched out, and weigh as much as thirty pounds. The average, however, should be somewhere between fifteen and twenty pounds, and the hen bird will weigh five pounds less. The old gobbler wears dark but brilliant iridescent colors that show up at their best in the sunlight. The hen bird wears more somber browns. The color, however, is not a good feature on which to rely for separating hens from gobblers. In the shadowy light of dawn in the deep woods, identification of the sexes is sometimes difficult, especially if a young gobbler comes into range.

But spring hunting regulations generally limit legal birds to gobblers with "beards." The beards are specialized feathers that hang down in a tassel from the front of the breast. Younger toms have shorter beards, but the old birds may wear them as much as a foot long. Occasionally hens will have small beards.

Fall hunting is preferred by some turkey hunters. Some even insist that spring gobbler hunting requires little skill. These hunters prefer the season when turkeys are assembled in family flocks feeding and living together. Here the turkey dog may come into use. Hunters and their dogs locate a flock of turkeys, and the dog is released to flush the birds. Then he is called back and tied up. Now the actual hunt begins. The skilled turkey callers begin talking to the birds,

The sharp eyes of the wild turkey, and his native wariness, make it essential for the hunter to hide himself and conduct his hunt with extreme caution. This hunter is camouflaged both with a camouflage suit and a brush blind. *By George Laycock.*

attempting to bring them back into gun range to the place from which they scattered. Sometimes it works. Biologists defend the spring hunts on the basis of selective hunting when it is easier to take the gobblers which have already performed their mating tasks. And no matter what anyone says, on a spring gobbler hunt the old bird has so many advantages that he is seldom taken easily even if he is in love.

Turkey hunters look for the signs revealing the presence of the birds. The leaves of the forest floor are often scratched up where the birds have uncovered acorns and beechnuts in their feeding. Their large droppings tell where they have traveled. If there is a snow the big tracks show where the birds have walked, while the disturbed snow sometimes reveals where they landed as they flew down from their roosts in an evergreen tree.

The killing of a wild turkey calls for a substantial load of shot. In some states they may be hunted with either rifles or shotguns. In others, especially the more heavily populated states, only shotguns are legal for taking turkeys.

Because turkeys talk among themselves, they can be successfully called by skilled turkey hunters manipulating any one of many turkey calls. *By George Laycock.*

The wild turkey is a magnificent prize, and many of those who hunt these grand birds prefer to take them with shotguns. *By Erwin A. Bauer.*

The best shotgun for the job is a 12- or 16-gauge. Anything smaller is likely to be too small, especially on longer shots. The shot should be big—Sizes No. 2 or 4 are best, and shot should never be smaller than No. 6.

For use in those areas where either shotgun or rifle is legal, the best gun might be one that combines one shotgun barrel with a rifle barrel, and in recent times there has been increasing interest in such guns. The .410 shotguns combined with the .22-caliber rifle, however, are too small to be good turkey guns.

This is one bird which the hunter may take on the ground without being shunned by fellow shooters. When you get within sure range of a legal turkey—and you know he is a legal bird—take him. If he flies, there is still a good chance to take him with a fast, well-placed wing shot.

The old gobbler has amazing recuperative powers. Many a turkey hunter has stood for a moment congratulating himself only to see the stunned bird bounce up and make a clean escape. "As soon as he drops," Wayne Bailey once reminded me, "I run right over and jump on top of him and grab his feet."

The use of the turkey call is important. There are several types available. Old-time hunters have fashioned them from all manner of odd materials. In addition to the old favored box call, there are slate and stick calls, and plastic diaphragm mouth calls. The call most commonly used to bring in a gobbler in spring is the yelping call of the hen. Occasionally the gobbling call of the tom will work. In fall, the one most productive is the plaintive, single-syllable call of the young bird lost from the flock. It is important to learn the calls, then practice them to avoid sounding sour notes which might carry a warning to suspicious birds. If you are good at reproducing the call of a turkey, there is little to fear from using the call too much. You may not, however, always see or hear the gobbler approaching, and the movement involved in calling him may alert him.

When you do get a shot at a turkey, the best plan is to shoot at the head and neck. Try to put the head in the middle of the pattern. The large body of a turkey can successfully carry off a considerable load of shot, especially if you make the mistake of using shot too small for the job. Remember that a flying turkey can attain a good speed; turkeys have been clocked at 55 mph. If you have a choice, the full-choke barrel is usually the best bet.

The most common mistake beginning turkey hunters make on a spring gobbler hunt, according to Wayne, is to stay in one spot if there is no sign of birds in the vicinity. After a while, if there is no action, get out and start hiking until you make contact with a bird. Stop every once in a while and listen, especially in early morning. If you hear gobbling, find yourself a good secluded location and try the hen call. Give him time. If he responds, he will come prancing along at his own leisurely pace.

Some hunters prefer to hunt gobblers without the aid of a turkey call. In this case it is es-

pecially important to get into the hunting territory at least a day early to allow time for scouting and finding out where the turkeys are. Listen for their gobbling at the break of day; learn, if possible, where their roosting trees are located and where they spend their time when off the roost. Then move through the woodlands quietly enough that you do not disturb the turkeys in their daily habits—at least until you interrupt one's routine on opening morning.

Personally, I prefer hunting with a turkey call. Hearing the gobble of a true wild turkey is a memorable outdoor experience, and especially so when the old bird is replying to my call.

This old-time turkey call employs a hand-made wooden box scraping against a piece of slate. It is especially useful in spring gobbler hunts because it resembles the call of a hen turkey. *By George Laycock.*

Chapter 24

CROWS

Crows are doubtless more numerous today than they were in prehistoric times. The opening of the land and the coming of farm crops, waste grains, feedlots, and dumps ushered in a new age of plenty for the crow. And here was a wild creature fully capable of adapting his living habits to take advantage of the changes. The crow ranks high in intelligence in the world of wildlife, is elusive, sharp-eyed, and wary. He works closely with others of his kind in a collective defense against danger. All these traits sharpen the challenge for those who pursue him.

What's more, the grain-consuming crows are widely disliked by farmers. Consequently, those who hunt them are welcomed to most agricultural lands—even where "No Hunting" signs are posted, providing permission is asked first. Crows are widely dispersed over North America. Because they are generally unprotected by law, there is a year-round open season.

What's more, crows provide excellent training for the upland game seasons as well as a challenge in their own right. Those needing still more reasons for shooting crows sometimes suggest eating them. I consider this an extreme.

Several skills, including calling, use of decoys, camouflage, and stalking, come into the successful pursuit of these common big blackbirds. Crows are hunted by attracting them within range of a blind. Color, form, and motion can all give away the hunter's position to the sharp-eyed crow. It is important to remain motionless until the final moment as the birds come within range. The blind may be high, thick-growing weeds pulled over the position. Better concealment can usually be obtained by building a special blind. It should preferably be constructed or covered by natural materials at hand—weeds, cornstalks, brush—that will make it appear a part of the surroundings. Some hunters darken their faces and wear camouflage clothing in the blind.

Camouflage clothing should never have a shiny surface that might reflect the sunlight. A rough material works better, and one of the good ones is common burlap. Hunters frequently fashion their crow hunting suits from large feed bags. In winter, when there is need for a white suit to match the snow, sheets may be made into camouflage outfits. A large sheet may also serve as a blind.

Crows are usually attracted with decoys and calls. One good decoy is a large artificial owl, which can be purchased at sporting goods stores. Mounted owls work well. Set the decoys in a tree or on top of a pole near your blind. Surround the owl with a dozen or so decoy crows. Then hide and begin using the crow call to sound the "rallying" or fighting call to crows within hearing range. Electronic calls, using actual recordings of crows, are available—and highly effective.

Crows are successfully called from long distances by such electronic devices as this record player and loudspeaker. *By Wightman Electronics Inc.*

One especially good season for crow hunting is late summer. The young crows are at their maximum population levels and often lack the experience and wariness of the older birds. Early morning is often the best time of day for crow shooting. The crows leave their roosting area and fan out to feed. Here is shooting where the added shells from an autoloader or pump gun may come in handy because the shooting can get fast. Perhaps most crow hunting is done with 12- and 16-gauge shotguns and No. 6 shot. A full choke is a common choice, but there is variation in the thinking of crow hunters as proved by the methods employed by one of my crow hunting friends, Carl Lowrance of Tulsa, Oklahoma. Carl invariably carries a .410 into the blinds for crows. Most of his shots have to be at close range, but he likes to call crows right into treetop level. His choice is a wide open pattern from three-inch shells loaded with No. 9 shot. It is his contention that the 12-gauge makes too much noise to be as effective as the .410 in crow shooting, but even when using the .410 he finds it extremely difficult to score doubles because the birds are naturally wary.

To make his crow hunting blind Carl starts with a twenty-one-foot strip of burlap in the widest width he can purchase. Using a spray gun, he decorates the strip of burlap with black stripes. Next he applies splotches of color to match the dominant vegetation color where he is hunting—often a dead-grass brown. With the help of clamp-type clothes pins, he fastens the burlap up around the blind area by pinning it to saplings and branches. If it is a bright day he wants the blind in the shade, because in sunlight the sharp-eyed crows can spot shadows of hunters inside. He locates the fields, usually on peanut farms, where the crows are feeding within calling distance, then enters his blind well ahead of daylight.

When the crows come in to feed, Carl uses a crow call to talk to them. Around him are about a hundred decoys, some on the ground, others in the trees. It is not unusual for him to take several dozen crows in a half day's shooting. Hunting alone, he once shot 178 crows between eleven o'clock in the morning and four o'clock in the afternoon.

Chapter 25

DUCK HUNTING

There was a thin film of ice across the shallow mud flat, and our insulated rubber boots shattered it noisily as we sloshed toward our blind out on the point. Half an hour ahead of the first light we were settled, our guns resting beside us, a Thermos of coffee nearby, and our senses tuned to the slightest sound. In front of the blind a dozen decoys rode quietly on the ripples. There were three of us, if you counted Jim the Labrador retriever, whose black coat made him totally invisible as he sat expectantly in his corner of the blind.

The first to come were two mallards, but they flew high and ignored the call. Twenty minutes passed. The morning came on gray and cold, and the wind carried occasional flakes of icy snow. Then we saw eight mallards coming in at an elevation of about five hundred feet. Their path carried them directly toward us.

Len, one of our group, let them get almost above us; then he spoke to them on his duck call. They flew another hundred yards and wheeled. They circled back for another look, as beautifully as you could ask, then settled in tight little descending circles to come down and join our decoys. The ducks, still not sensing their peril, were scarcely ten feet off the water. We both stood at once. Seconds later Jim was splashing joyously through the shallow water to bring the two big mallards back to the blind. It was a scene that never grows old for a waterfowl hunter.

In spite of the fact that waterfowl populations are no longer as big as they once were—and are likely never to be again—there are still opportunities for those who want to hunt ducks. In some areas, the natural waters attracting ducks have been supplemented by farm ponds and reservoirs. Several states have established shooting areas that are managed for waterfowl hunting. On some of the National Wildlife Refuges set aside especially for management of waterfowl, hunters find duck and goose shooting ranking with the best anywhere. A directory of these refuges is found in my book *The Sign of the Flying Goose.* * A check with your state game and fish agency will reveal whether or not there are public hunting areas in your state. Your local game protector knows where you can obtain such information if he doesn't have it himself.

Consistent success in duck hunting calls for understanding the birds' habits, beginning with their migratory patterns. In a general way, it can be said that ducks nest in the North and fly south for the winter. It can also be said that there are four major waterfowl flyways: Atlantic, Mississippi, Central, and Pacific. Within these flyways are definite routes, or flight paths, followed by various species and flocks.

The ducks of North America are commonly divided into two groups, the puddle ducks and the divers. About twenty species of diving ducks appear in North America, and about sixteen

One related interest followed by some duck hunters is collecting old decoys, such as the one shown here. *By George Laycock.*

* The Natural History Press, a division of Doubleday & Company, Inc., 1965.

These hunters near Stuttgart, Arkansas, typically wade through the flooded Oak River bottomlands where the mallards concentrate in great numbers. *By George Laycock.*

The duck call, skillfully used, can bring birds within range of the shotgunner. *By George Laycock.*

species of puddle ducks are found on the continent.

The puddle ducks are found on inland fresh waters, often in the shallow water areas. Among them are the mallard, black duck, pintail, wood duck, teal, widgeon, gadwall, and shoveler.

The diving ducks seek out the deeper waters, both inland and along the coasts. They normally dive deeply for their food, while the puddle ducks simply tip up and dabble around in the shallows to feed. The divers include the canvasback, redhead, scaup, ring-necked duck, ruddy, goldeneye, bufflehead, and mergansers or "fish ducks."

Of the two groups, the puddle ducks are generally better to eat than those of the diving group, with the possible exception of the redhead and canvasback.

Accurate waterfowl identification is important and likely to become increasingly so because the trend in hunting regulations is toward what the waterfowl biologists refer to as "species management." As some species become rare, there are often special regulations protecting them. Here

An eager and obedient dog such as this black Lab is usually essential to the successful duck hunter. *By Erwin A. Bauer.*

recognition of the ducks found in the hunter's flyway becomes essential. The burden of identification rests on the shooter. Various bird books are helpful. The U. S. Fish and Wildlife Service has an excellent illustrated pamphlet for twenty-five cents entitled, "Ducks at a Distance."

Puddle ducks rise from the water by lifting themselves straight upward as if spring-propelled. Divers, on the other hand, gain their takeoff speed gradually, often beating their feet and wings along the surface of the water as they gain speed.

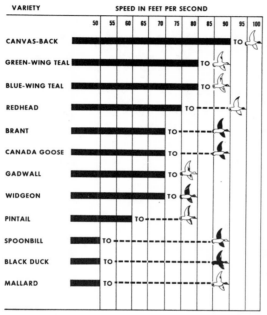

Speeds of various waterfowl. *By Winchester-Western.*

Any ducks feeding on farmlands are most likely puddle ducks. These ducks generally possess more colorful wing patches than the diving ducks. Experienced duck hunters learn other features that help them identify the waterfowl species, including how they form flocks, the speed with which the wings beat, what the silhouettes look like, and how the ducks call.

Waterfowl seasons are the subject of heated discussions every year in meetings across the country. Because waterfowl are migratory, they are an international resource. The same ducks that you see in the United States may spend part of the year in Canada and Mexico as well. Biologists survey the duck production in the northern prairie potholes and marshes each year.

They make recommendations on how many days of duck hunting there shall be and what special rules must be observed on various species. Then the individual states establish their duck hunting regulations within this prescribed framework. The hunter learns the dates and regulations from his local newspaper or radio. He can call his county game protector for the latest information or write to his state conservation department in the state capital.

The first requirements for duck hunting are *both* a hunting license and a waterfowl hunting stamp. The duck stamp is obtainable from post offices across the country at a cost of a few dollars. This is a federal stamp, good anywhere with appropriate state licenses. A new waterfowl stamp is required each year. The money goes for a good purpose—the purchase and management of wetlands. Money from the duck stamp has played a major role in establishing our federal waterfowl refuges.

There are some rules a hunter should remember when building a blind. Rule one is to make the

Among the modern inventions for the comfort and convenience of duck hunters is this combination seat and container for shells, lunch, and raingear. *By Woodstream Corp.*

Duck hunter shooting over decoys on the edge of a marsh. *By Winchester-Western.*

Among the several ways of hunting ducks is this method of stalking them employed by an Indiana hunter. He floated the river, spotted the ducks well ahead, and took to the shore to approach them. *By George Laycock.*

blind blend into its surroundings. Use materials that are found in the area. Blinds are frequently camouflaged with grasses and brush, but these should look as though they belong there. They should not, however, be gathered from the area adjacent to the blind because this harvesting in itself can change the character of the landscape.

The framework of a blind, as well as the covering, can be constructed in a wide variety of ways. One common method is to wrap chicken wire around poles driven into the marsh. Then weave native dead grasses into the wire. Fish netting will substitute for chicken wire. Burlap makes a good covering where it blends into the surroundings.

There are times and places where the natural cover provides all the blind the hunter needs. This may be true beside the cattail-fringed farm pond, or the rocky, boulder-strewn shoreline.

Some duck hunters forsake the fixed blind for a chance to float for ducks on the rivers. By camouflaging a boat or canoe it is sometimes possible to drift into shooting range of ducks, especially when streams are high and hunters can invade the backwaters of flooded bottom-lands.

There is not much doubt that the most popular waterfowling gun is the 12-gauge, with barrels that are either modified or full choke depending on the kind of hunting the shooter normally practices. For pass shooting, where the birds are sometimes taken at rather long range, the full-choke barrel is in order, and the modified

can serve well when shooting over decoys. On occasion, I have seen duck hunters do a creditable job with their .410s. But this does not influence me at all in favor of the little guns for waterfowl. This is a time to leave the job to the bigger guns and high-velocity loads. Pump guns and autoloaders are popular with duck hunters. Waterfowl hunters are limited to three shells in the gun.

Too often shooters, especially the less-experienced ones, try for the long shots on ducks. At best they miss them, and at worst they cripple them as well as reap the curses of other shooters in nearby blinds.

Magnum loads increase the density of shot in a pattern, but waterfowl hunters should not assume that magnums enable them to make killing shots at abnormally long ranges.

Some years ago Winchester-Western, working with the Illinois Natural History Survey, carried out a research project to determine how fewer ducks might be lost by crippling. They were comparing the relative effectiveness of No. 4 and No. 6 shot for waterfowl. They checked both at ranges of thirty-five, forty, fifty, and sixty-five yards. The size of the shot seemed to make little difference at the closer range of thirty-five yards. But as the range increased, the percentage of cripples with No. 6 shot increased more rapidly than it did with No. 4s. The larger shot reached out with more impact. Their conclusion was that for duck shooting at ranges of forty yards and beyond the No. 4 shot are superior to No. 6s.

Modern high-grade decoys are frequently made of plastic, light in weight and realistic. *By Woodstream Corp.*

Chapter 26

GEESE

Ahead of daylight three of us picked our way through the muddy field of corn stubble. Cold rain beat steadily against our rubber garments. We were equipped with shotguns, shells, and coffee. And we had permits to hunt that November day in one of the big pit blinds on Kentucky's famous Ballard County Waterfowl Area.

We stored our gear under the abbreviated roof of the blind, then hurried to collect extra cornstalks and weeds to camouflage it. The blind had been well constructed. All we had to do now was wait tensely for daylight and the birds—in this case geese.

The Canada goose is top prize in the waterfowl hunter's world, a trophy bird anywhere, and choice fare on the banquet table. In recent times this bird has become the central figure in one of the most successful wildlife management efforts in North America. Consequently, the hunter's chances of getting within shooting range of one of these fine big birds are considerably better today than they have been for several decades.

In addition to the Canada geese which North American shotgunners pursue, there are the blue geese, snow geese, and white-fronted geese, all of which are important waterfowl to hunters in various sections of the country. Ross's geese, which show up in California, are found in limited numbers. Brant are small, dark, sea geese found along the coasts.

Various races of Canada geese range in size from a little four-pound cackling goose to the biggest of the clan, the giant Canada goose, which may reach fourteen pounds or more. The average Canada goose, which most of us might have an opportunity to bag, frequently falls in the eight- to nine-pound class. Following their nesting season in the north, geese work their way southward during autumn. During these travels along their traditional flyways, hunters have an opportunity to put a Christmas goose on the table.

There are four major waterfowl flyways within the United States. These are subdivided into other flyways which flocks of geese follow. The geese in the Mississippi Flyway, for example, are divided into three separate populations, each with its own nesting area and wintering grounds. One of these, perhaps better understood today than any other, is called the Mississippi Valley flock.

Not too many decades ago geese from this population moved all the way down the Mississippi Flyway. Some wintered in the coastal areas along the Gulf of Mexico. Then wildlife biologists learned that geese can be enticed by food and protection to alter their winter travel plans. By establishing refuges complete with plantings of grain and green crops, waterfowl managers can tempt geese out of the sky. Among the first wildlife biologists to understand this were specialists working for the state of Illinois.

In 1927, Illinois established its famous Horseshoe Lake Goose Management Area on thirty-five hundred acres of riverbottom land along the Mississippi. Then came other goose refuge areas managed on the same principle, some by states, and some by the U. S. Fish Wildlife Service.

Wintering flocks increased and brought unanticipated problems to some of these refuges. Around Wisconsin's Horicon Marsh there are sometimes so many geese that farmers' crops are threatened. Federal workers have even tried, unsuccessfully, to move these geese south by hazing them with helicopters.

On and around such refuges, hunters usually hide in pit blinds and wait for geese to fly over when passing between resting and feeding areas. The idea works best in bad weather. The dark night prevents the geese from flying to feed. When morning comes, the big birds are hungry. They leave the pond areas a few at a time. Gradually the exodus picks up. Soon the sky is filled with flocks of geese shifting from area to area.

Someplace across the half-dark refuge we could hear the calls of a little flock of geese moving out. Then we could see the line of birds on a path that should bring them over our blind. There was only one thing wrong; they were far too high to risk a shot. It's best to limit your shots to forty yards or so. Suddenly a volley of shots rang out from the blind on our right. We could see the dark forms of the birds flare against the gray sky and disperse in every direction.

These goose hunters finished their morning's hunt in western Kentucky with a limit bag of two birds each. *By George Laycock.*

Typical flock of Canada geese resting on a refuge pond. *By U. S. Fish and Wildlife Service.*

Well-equipped goose hunters with shotguns, binoculars, camouflage clothing, decoys, versatile field vehicle, and some of the geese and ducks taken. *By Erwin A. Bauer.*

Too often waterfowl shooters are tempted to fire away at birds that would be considered long distance even to a telephone operator. This practice seldom puts birds on the table or endears the shooter to fellow hunters in neighboring blinds. To discourage such one-man early warning systems for geese, some refuges limit the number of shells a hunter can carry into the blind. In Kentucky's Ballard Area, where hunters are allowed two Canada geese, the limit is ten shells. When they're gone, you're done.

Under most circumstances, the best gun for goose shooting is the 12-gauge full choke.

The goose is a rugged animal, and far too many are carrying lead souvenirs from the guns of hunters who chose the wrong loads for the job, or could not resist those impossibly high shots. Favorite loads among seasoned goose shooters are high-base shells with No. 2 or No. 4 shot. Some hunters use a load of No. 6 shot with a load of No. 4 as a follow-up. Generally, this is a job for the larger sizes, and BB shot is not out of place in the goose blind. Magnum loads are a good choice for goose shooting whether in standard 2¾-inch shells, or three-inch shells in those guns chambered for the longer sizes.

The sharp-eyed old goose or gander from the advantage of its high altitude quickly spots unusual objects in the world below. A hunter's face staring up from a hole in the blind does not instill confidence in wild geese. This is a time for hunters to stay hidden. Some hunters stand up in the blind, then duck down at what they take to be the last moment. Usually they have already been spotted.

Choice of clothing is important for two reasons. The weather is often wet or bitterly cold, or both. Outfit yourself with a good rain suit, heavy clothing, and a good pair of boots. And, because geese might otherwise spot you more easily, select clothing of somber colors—an outfit that blends into the surroundings.

What about goose calls? The first rule should be to learn to use one properly if you plan to carry it. Too many goose hunters honk away on a call far more than they should. Poorly used calls alert birds to the fact that something is unnatural down there. And hunters in nearby pits get unhappy about it too.

Geese coming into an area to feed can be attracted by decoys. They can often be fooled by surprisingly ungoose-like forms—anything from paper bags staked to the ground, to cones of

The magnificent Canada goose is a prize trophy becoming increasingly common for shotgunners in many parts of the country. *By U. S. Fish and Wildlife Service.*

chicken wire covered with white cloth. Many goose shooters use silhouettes cut from plywood, painted in goose patterns and colors, and stuck into the ground around the blind. Other hunters purchase more lifelike decoys from a sporting goods store. A dozen should do the job. Some public shooting areas supply the decoys already placed in front of the pits.

Geese come to any one of a wide variety of decoys, such as this silhouette. *By Woodstream Corp.*

This full-bodied plastic goose decoy has interchangeable stands to indicate various attitudes such as sentinel, resting, and feeding. *By Woodstream Corp.*

Chapter 27

WOODCOCK AND RAILS

WOODCOCK

By many standards the woodcock is a strange-looking bird of unusual habits. Many hunters would scarcely recognize one if they encountered it, but estimates of the number taken each year come to nearly half a million. The seasons are usually long.

The woodcock, or "timber doodle," is content to remain secluded in the shadows of the thickets during the daylight hours. He comes out in the hours of darkness to do his feeding. Only recently have research biologists begun to gain a better understanding of the woodcock's way of life. The most detailed study of this bird has been completed under the guidance of Dr. William G. Sheldon, leader of the Massachusetts Cooperative Wildlife Research Unit.

Here is a bird eminently fitted for his perpetual search for earthworms. He harvests them from the fertile, moist soil beneath thickets of such plants as alder, aspen, birch, and black locust. There, hidden from the rest of the world, the woodcock uses his four-inch-long bill to probe in the earth. The holes are revealing evidence to hunters seeking new woodcock territory. On occasion the birds also leave the moist thickets to wander through upland fields and pick up side dishes of insects.

There are disconcerting moments in the hunting of the woodcock when the bird sticks tight until you walk within inches of him squatting in the shadows. Then, whistling as he rises, the woodcock often goes straight up before leveling off and gaining speed in his erratic escape flight.

Some woodcock, it is now known, migrate, while others apparently remain in their home territories. A freeze-up can seal off their food supplies and send them southward.

The female is about one-third larger than the male, and in the hand can be separated from the male by the wider wing and longer bill.

Small shot are needed for woodcock. They should never be larger than No. 7½, and preferably should be No. 9. Hold off on shooting until the bird gains a little range. Too often the fast-shooting hunter not accustomed to the woodcock's takeoff shoots too soon. Either he misses because of the small, tight pattern, or he destroys the bird.

CLAPPER RAILS

Since colonial days, hunting the clapper rail, or "marsh hen," has been a favorite sport in the tidal marshes along the coasts of eastern and southern states. They are found in salt-water marshes from Connecticut southward around the coast of the continent. In some sections the rail hunters are a select minority of the hunting fraternity, and there are birds enough for more hunters who want to invade the salt marshes. There are, for example, New Jersey marshes in the southern part of that populous state where clapper rail hunting offers more sporting opportunities than most hunters realize.

The woodcock is usually found in moist areas where it probes for earthworms, its favorite food. *By George Laycock.*

These rails, with their wingspread of about twenty inches, seem large when they rise from marsh grass, but their weight is less than a pound, usually much less. They are equipped with long legs and long beaks, and their bodies, "as thin as a rail," enable them to slip through the vegetation easily and without commotion. They feed largely on snails and crabs.

The clapper rail is hunted in several ways. Some hunters walk them up, either with or without the aid of a dog. Some organize into lines and march through the marsh clapping their hands and yelling, to bring the birds up on the wing. But the best-known method is for two hunters to go out in a shallow-draft boat and pole through the marsh vegetation. One poles while the other shoots, and they take turns.

Tides play a big role in the success of hunting the clapper rail. Experienced hunters watch the timetables for high tides. When there is an especially high tide, the flooding of the lowlands forces the rails into the highest points of the marsh. Meanwhile, the added water enables the boats to approach the birds.

Saltwater can be hard on metals, and consequently marsh hunters often use an old shotgun they are not too concerned about in case it gets dampened with salt spray. No. 8 shot is a good size for clapper rails.

SORA RAILS

The little sora rail, which nests in fresh-water marshes from Canada to Pennsylvania, provides hunting which can be confusing at times but not highly exciting. This is an elusive little bird, with a short beak and thin body. He prefers to hide

In most areas the woodcock is lightly hunted. It is, however, an unusual and sometimes elusive target. *By George Laycock.*

in the thick-growing vegetation and, once flushed, executes a weak, low-level flight that seldom takes him very far. He lifts himself to the top of the cattails, and with both legs dangling beneath him, flutters off in a straight and level flight that may end before you expect it. Just as you shoot, the little sora may manage a pancake landing into the thick-growing vegetation and try to escape on foot.

Small guns and small shot are at their best in this brand of hunting. Use No. 9 shot, and let the rail get out as far as you dare before shooting. Then retrieve him at once. Here is where a good dog comes into the plan, because the sora is exceptionally hard to spot in a tangle of vegetation, which more often than not blends with his camouflage.

In many parts of its original range the sora rail has become the victim of drainage schemes and various kinds of pollution. These forces are far more devastating to the population than the hunter's take.

Chapter 28

DEER

Deer have staged a surprising comeback from those bleak days around the turn of the century. Devastating timbering practices combined with land-ruining farming techniques, and plain over-shooting, decimated the forest game. Along with the turkeys, bear, and elk, the whitetail deer had disappeared from one eastern state after another. Few people ever expected to see them living wild again in such places as Ohio, and some other heavily populated areas. But in recent times there have been legal open seasons on deer in all fifty states.

Improved forestry practices let the timberlands return to productivity, and the deer came back and adjusted to life on and around man's holdings. In areas where they did not yet prosper, game managers frequently live-trapped them from

areas of abundance, and turned them free to start new populations in areas where deer were scarce or absent.

The happy result was a bright new age for deer hunting. Through much of the range, however, people had become so abundant that the thought of turning hunters lose in the woodlands with high-powered rifles frightened officials. Shotguns seemed potentially less dangerous to the community at large. Consequently shotguns have become standard deer guns in large segments of the land. There are some areas, such as the southeastern states, where they have always been preferred for deer hunting.

But the shotgun, in the hands of a good hunter, can put venison in the locker year after year. It is actually superior to a rifle for hunting deer in thick cover where the gun must be handled fast, and the charge may have to rip through considerable vegetation to reach its destination.

Which shotguns are suitable for deer hunting? Generally, only the larger gauges—the 12s and 16s—should be used on these big-game animals. It is not that you can't get ammunition for the smaller bores. No problem there. There are deer loads available even for the .410 shotgun, al-

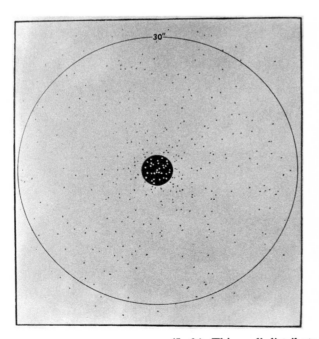
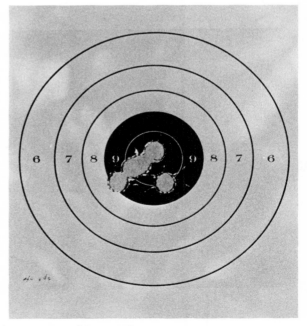

(Left) This well-distributed pattern at thirty yards was delivered by an Ithaca Deerslayer especially made for rifled slugs, but in this case shooting No. 7½ shot. (Right) The same gun delivered, at forty yards, this group of five slugs in a 1¾-inch pattern. *By Ithaca Gun Co.*

though it is difficult for me to see why. This little gun is definitely out of its league in the deer woods. Most deer hunters likewise consider the 20-gauge too light for deer hunting.

To understand what is asked of a shotgun in the deer woods, take a look at the ammunition available. Unless you live in an area where the use of buckshot on deer is traditional (and legal), you will use shells carrying a single rifled slug. The rifled slug is a ball of soft lead, light in back and heavy in front—a fact of design which helps to keep it from tumbling over and over. In addition, the rifled slug is made with spiral lands and grooves designed to influence it to maintain a spinning motion.

The slug for a 12-gauge gun weighs one ounce, for a 20-gauge, ⅝ ounce, and for a .410 it takes five slugs to weigh an ounce. The effectiveness of one of these slugs is determined largely by the foot-pounds of energy it carries at various ranges from the muzzle. The figures fall off rapidly for the smaller guns, making them less effective at ranges where the 12-gauge might score nicely. In any case, the shotgun is not suitable for long shots. A large percentage of deer taken with slugs are shot at ranges under fifty yards. Most experienced hunters consider seventy-five yards a long shot.

The first-time deer hunter, and sometimes the more experienced one as well, should purchase some extra rifled slugs well ahead of the season. Set up a practice target and fire enough rounds to know what a slug from your shotgun will do at various distances. These chunks of lead drop rapidly while still relatively short distances from the muzzle. At fifty yards the slug from a 2¾-

One much-practiced method of deer hunting, especially in areas of thick cover where close shots are called for, is waiting at a crossing where deer are expected to come through. *By George Laycock.*

Big buck taken in northeastern Ohio with single rifled slug. *By George Laycock*.

inch 12-gauge can be expected to drop 2.1 inches, and at one hundred yards it will have fallen 10.4 inches.

By using a large paper target, a shotgunner can soon tell how far to left or right of the mark his gun throws a slug. Then by shooting enough rounds at measured twenty-five, fifty, seventy-five, and one-hundred-yard distances, he begins to understand how much drop he must compensate for in field shooting. This is also important in instilling a better understanding of distance. The ability to estimate distance becomes highly important, especially if you attempt shots at deer more than fifty yards away. Practice until you can

put slugs into a circle the size of a pie pan consistently at measured distances. The shells are not costly when you consider the costs of travel and licenses involved in a deer-hunting trip.

Most deer hunters going forth with shotgun and slugs will carry the gun they use for other kinds of game. The soft lead slugs, incidentally, do not damage the choke of a shotgun. If, however, you should consider purchase of a shotgun primarily for deer hunting, there are a few good points to bear in mind. For most gunners the single-barrel, or the over-and-under-double is a better choice for deer. It is not enough to just point at a deer and expect the pattern to do the

This Ohio deer hunter surprised a buck from his bed within easy range of the rifled slug carried in his autoloading shotgun. *By George Laycock.*

Slug sleeve designed by Williams Gun Sight Co. to add distance to effective shotgun range for deer hunters. *By Williams Gun Sight Co.*

job because there isn't any pattern. There is a need for aiming.

Although choke in the barrel of a shotgun is not damaged by shooting rifled slugs, these loads are more effectively shot from barrels bored with little or no choke. In recent times arms manufacturers, taking notice of the growing fraternity of shotgun-carrying deer hunters, began marketing shotguns built especially for shooting slugs. First came Ithaca with its Deerslayer. Soon other manufacturers offered barrels bored especially for effective shooting of slugs.

Depending on which shotgun you already own, it may be possible to purchase a deer-hunting barrel interchangeable with the standard barrel you use for upland game or waterfowl. Owners of Ithaca automatics with serial numbers over 855,000 can order a Deerslayer barrel interchangeable without additional factory adjustment. Remington offers a deer-hunter's barrel in 12-

gauge along with a selection of other interchangeable barrels for its Model 870 pump gun, as well as its Model 11-48, and Model 1100 autoloaders. Outdoorsmen who own Winchester Model 1200 pump guns, or Model 1400 autoloaders in 12-gauge can purchase special interchangeable deer-hunting barrels for these guns also.

Today a deer hunter can buy rifled slugs in two general types. The ones most commonly carried are made either by Remington or Winchester, and they are much alike. They have a weight of 404 grains in 12-gauge and are offered in 2¾-inch shot shells. As for muzzle velocity, they check out at sixteen hundred feet per second. In shape the slug is a bullet with a blunted nose. The back is hollowed out to give it greater weight forward.

It was hunter Karl Foster who, in the early 1930s, turned out the first such slugs in his Massachusetts shop. He had cut spiraled lands and grooves into the slug in an effort to improve on the old "punkinball." The idea was first utilized commercially by Winchester in 1936.

In addition, there is the Brenneke slug, which is imported from Germany. It is also rifled, but it carries a shape considerably different from that of domestically made rifled slugs. Both are heavier in front. The Brenneke, with a weight in 12-gauge of 491 grains, is considerably heavier than the 404-grain slugs in domestically made shot-shells of the same gauge. From a practical point of view, the average deer hunter has less trouble finding Remington or Winchester-Western shells. Which slug he chooses may be far less important, however, than the test shooting and practice he does before the season opens.

For complete details on deer hunting, see *The Deer Hunter's Bible*.

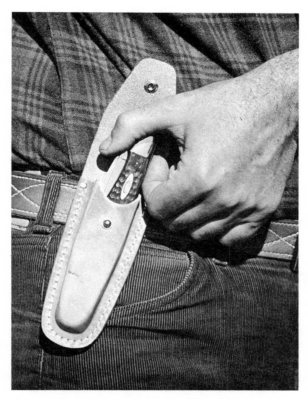

Among the extra equipment with which the deer hunter should provide himself is a good skinning knife. *By George Laycock*.

Chapter 29

GUN SAFETY

No matter where you see them, the rules for safe gun handling always read as if you have seen them before, about fifty times. This stands to reason, because chances are you have, and there is precious little anyone can say about gun safety that is new or surprising.

Summed up, it all comes out, "Don't make any damn fool careless mistakes or you're going to be sorry whether you're here to know about it or not."

Gun safety has its beginning in two places, a knowledge of your firearms, and a mature, deliberate approach in handling them. A good gun handler will not be seen horsing around with a gun. He has full control over both his emotions and his firearm. He's the steady type, dependable, deliberate, self-assured. He knows where the end of the gun is pointing at any time, and how to make the gun do what he expects of it. He knows it because he has studied the firearm and practiced with it. His confidence promotes safe gun handling.

But the old safety rules for gun handlers are never out of style. Here are points to remember:

Have your shotgun unloaded when you are transporting or storing it, climbing a fence, tree, or ledge, jumping a ditch, awaiting your turn on a shooting line, or approaching an occupied area.

See that barrel and action are not obstructed.

Keep the safety on until ready to shoot.

Don't shoot at something you haven't positively identified.

Skip the alcohol until after the hunt or the shooting is finished.

Do not mix shells of different gauges.

This youthful hunter has learned that the muzzle should never be pointed at anything he does not want to shoot. *By Savage Arms Co.*

Carry the shotgun so that it is always under full control and the muzzle is pointed away from other hunters. *By Savage Arms Co.*

This 16-gauge autoloader barrel exploded because it was blocked with a piece of cleaning cloth. *By George Laycock.*

Twelve-gauge shotguns have sometimes blown up, as did this one, by having a 20-gauge shell stuck in the barrel while loading and firing a 12-gauge shell. *By George Laycock.*

It is good practice to inspect shotgun barrels for possible obstructions. The shotgun action should be open when one is not actually hunting and when one is around other people. *By Savage Arms Co.*

Gun cases should be considered essential for shotguns. In some places the law requires that all guns be cased when carried in vehicles. A gunsmith I talk with often, recently told me about a 12-gauge that was brought to his shop. He did not remember what service the shooter wanted him to perform. That was not the point of his story. As he does all incoming guns, he inspected the barrel and chamber. In the barrel was a small piece of waste material from the cheap gun case. "That," the gunsmith assured me, "would have been enough to blow up the barrel."

Each autumn when gun clubs become especially active just ahead of the approaching hunting season, one gunsmith, Charley Grossman of Milford, Ohio, digs into the recesses of his shop and brings out his prime examples of what carelessness can do to the gun owner. He carries out to the front of the shop two shotgun barrels which have one thing in common—they have both blown up.

One is a 12-gauge Savage autoloader. The owner got in trouble when he mistakenly slipped a 20-gauge shell into the breech, forgot it, and followed it with a 12-gauge. The smaller shell lodged in the barrel. The 12-gauge shell fired.

The 20-gauge, which did not even fire, is still lodged in what's left of the barrel. The accident cost the shooter one hand.

The other barrel is from a 16-gauge Remington 11-48. The owner of this one cleaned the gun but inadvertently left a patch of cloth stuck in the barrel. "What shooters should realize," Charley said holding the gun barrel up where I could see it, "is that the barrel does not have to be completely obstructed to cause a blowup." The 16-gauge blew apart in the middle. Although the owner escaped serious injury, he lost a gun and perhaps a few nights' sleep remembering the event.

Often I have wondered if a shotgun shell would explode from the force of dropping it. The only instance of this I've heard of occurred in the home of an acquaintance who took up reloading, largely against his wife's wishes. One day, while cleaning around the shop, his wife knocked off a box of the reloads. They scattered around her feet, and one of them hit the primer just right (or just wrong) and exploded. Although she suffered no noticeable bodily injury, the event did bring an abrupt end to reloading in that household.

 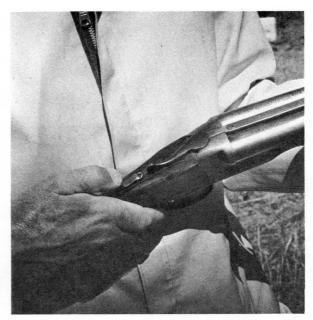

These two photos show two common types of safety device provided on shotguns: (left) a crossbolt safety placed behind the trigger and easily reached by the shooter's forefinger; (right) a tang-type safety easily worked by the shooter's thumb. In either case the safety should be on except when the gun is being mounted for a shot. *By George Laycock.*

If you travel a commercial airline with your firearms, you must, by federal regulations, case the guns before boarding—a sensible protection for both guns and people.

Surprisingly, gun owners sometimes use their firearms as clubs to beat brush for flushing game or to subdue cripples. One still reads every autumn of hunters whose last mortal act is pulling a gun through a fence, muzzle first. Others leave the safety off and accidentally fire the gun. Some use the barrels for prying open gates and doors, or fail to inspect the muzzle for foreign materials such as snow or mud. There are many ways to get into trouble with a gun. Most people, however, understand their guns and appreciate their responsibility with them.

Chapter 30

SHIPPING YOUR SHOTGUN

There may come a time in the life of any shotgun when it becomes necessary for the owner to return it to the factory for service. The big gun companies get thousands of guns into their service departments every year.

Recently the service manager of one of the major gun companies told me that his department logs in twenty-two thousand guns annually. About half of these are shotguns. The department tries to have each gun repaired and shipped off again within a week. Not all cases, however, are that simple.

How should you pack a gun for shipment? One service manager guided me over to a hand truck stacked high with incoming guns. For the most part they were well-packed. A few were in wooden boxes made by the owner. Unless such a box is secured with screws, some companies ordinarily return the gun in a new cardboard carton. The cardboard is adequate protection, and shipping costs are lower.

Most gun owners pack their shotguns in cardboard boxes, protected by crumpled newspapers or other packing materials. The boxes are taped or tightly tied. The preferred method of shipping is by parcel post. The gun package should be insured. There should be a letter of instructions attached to the outside of the box. "We like to get as much detailed information as possible about the trouble," one service manager explained. "If a person simply says that it is defective, we don't know what kind of trouble he is experiencing."

Strangely enough, a good number of guns going back to service departments have nothing wrong with them. One gun came back with a letter stating that, "This shotgun won't hit a tree if you walk up to it and bang the barrel against the trunk. I shot it," the letter added, "cousin Ben shot it, and Uncle John shot it, and it won't hit anything." The service department test-fired it and promptly found out three things: the owner was a bad shot, cousin Ben was a bad shot, and Uncle John was a bad shot. The gun fired perfectly.

Unless you know specifically what the trouble is with your gun, return the entire shotgun to the service department when shipping it in for repairs. The service people will probably want to test-fire it after repairs are made.

Among the jobs factory gunsmiths can perform is reboring for a more open choke. If you want your gun barrel changed from full choke to modified to improved cylinder, the boring can be done for as little as five to seven dollars.

Few developments can shake up a service department more than opening a package to find a loaded gun. Unbelievably, quite a number of guns returned to service departments arrive loaded, and some even carry a live shell in the chamber. One large manufacturer told me they received about forty loaded guns annually. Most of these are .22 rifles. It has, however, happened with such guns as shotguns and even 30-06s. For this reason the service department usually opens incoming packages in a special stall with laminated walls made from layers of wood and lead. Such shipping of guns, of course, is contrary to postal regulations as well as all the rules of common sense. There is no excuse.

The largest shipments of incoming shotguns arrive just ahead of the hunting season. This puts a burden on the gunsmiths. The owner also runs the risk of not having his favorite gun on

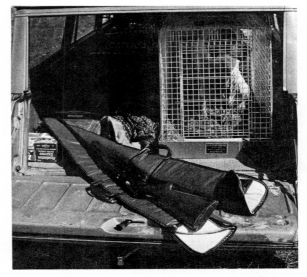

Guns should be protected during travel. *By Bill Boatman Co.*

opening day. If your gun requires work, try shipping it during less frantic spring and summer months. Service departments will make estimates of repair costs for gun owners requesting them. Manufacturers, incidentally, restrict their gun work to guns from their own factories.

The causes of troubles with guns shipped back to factories could be listed in wide variety. Frequently, a shotgun will come back with a bent or dented barrel. Gun owners often consider the gun barrel indestructible. "But this is a hollow tube of fairly soft steel," one service manager told me, "and it deserves careful handling." A gun owner once complained to the manufacturer because his gun barrel bent when he substituted it for a jack handle. Gun barrels are frequently bent by being backed over by a car or tractor, and sometimes by being mishandled in the hunting camp.

Guns often arrive in service departments amaz-ingly dirty. Barrels are clogged with the nests of mud daubers, and actions choked with chaff and hayseed. A good cleaning can often put such a gun in fine working condition without sending it back for factory service.

Occasionally a barrel will burst. One of the most frequent causes is a mix-up of 20- and 12-gauge shells. The 20-gauge shell will lodge ahead of the chamber, leaving room for the 12-gauge. Both shells fire at once, and the result is a little much to ask of the average shotgun. Amazingly, most such accidents permit the shooter to escape injury-free. But the event does nothing to improve the shape of a shotgun. With the new color-coded shells, this type of accident should become increasingly rare.

It is against postal regulations to mail ammunition. It should be shipped by express instead. Service departments do not need, nor usually want your ammunition along with the gun.

Chapter 31

SHOTGUN CARE

In the old farmhouse which some of us can recall, every item had its special place. The cat slept in front of the fireplace, the coal oil lamp rested on the mantel, and the 12-gauge was always behind the kitchen door, handy when Dad had to bound outdoors to ward off a "chicken" hawk. (All hawks were chicken hawks in those days.)

Nobody worried too much about taking care of a shotgun, however. It was usually cleaned once a year with the first load of No. 6s to rattle through it after rabbit season opened.

Even so, it seldom if ever failed its owner. But the fact remains that a shotgun—even an old one parked behind the kitchen door—deserves a little more in the way of care and grooming. A lifetime of dependable service from a shotgun calls for following a few simple rules in taking care of it.

It is true that guns need less care today than back in the black powder age. Black powder plus the old mercuric primers tended to crust the bore with accumulated residues of metal and carbon. Then came smokeless powders and priming mixtures that no longer caused corrosion. Consequently, gun cleaning became considerably less of a chore.

Shotguns need to be cleaned properly inside and outside on occasion. And the actions should be cleaned and lightly lubricated now and then. This can be especially important with the gas-actuated autoloaders, where too much dirt or oil

Good field care of a gun calls for occasional inspection, wiping moisture and dirt from it, and checking barrel for obstruction. *By George Laycock.*

can make the action balk and sometimes cause the shooter to miss the opportunity for an important follow-up shot.

Equipment and supplies needed for gun cleaning can be purchased for five or six dollars. The best cleaning rod is one that does not bring metal parts into contact with the inside of the gun barrel. This may be an easily stored, jointed wooden rod or one coated with some nonmetallic material. It should have a screw-threaded tip that can be fitted with two or three different cleaning attachments.

In addition to this kind of cleaning equipment, which is usually kept at home for use after you come from the field, you can, if you wish, purchase a compact field kit for a few dollars. Such a kit fits hunting coat or back pack and can be useful when on prolonged hunting trips.

In addition to the rod and tips, you will need wool swabs or balls for the inside of the gun, a slotted metal gun patch attachment, and perhaps a brass cleaning brush. Then you should have a good solvent for cleaning the inside of the gun barrel, plus a light, high-quality gun oil for the

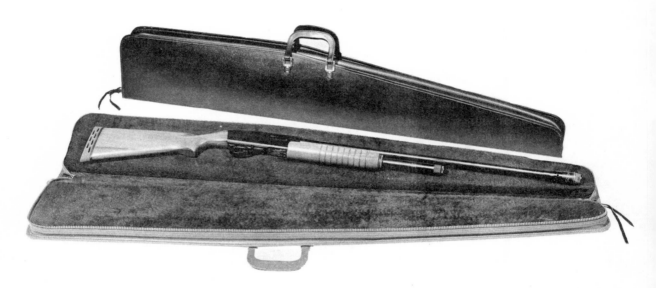

A rigid but well-padded gun case such as this provides good protection for shotguns carried by traveling shooters. *By Haralco, Inc.*

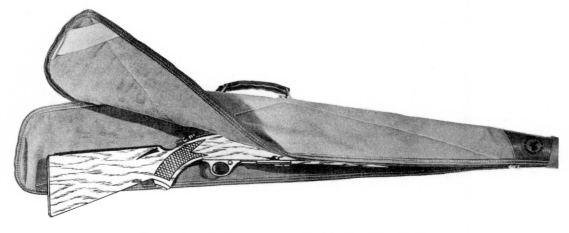

Zippered protective gun case. *By Marble Arms Corp.*

Occasional attention with a shotgun cleaning kit is all that is needed to keep most shotguns in good shooting order. *By Bill Boatman Co.*

metal parts. For the gunstock you may want an additional container of special gun wax or linseed oil. Oil made for metal parts should not be used on the stock.

The process in cleaning a shotgun is simple. First, run a clean flannel patch through the barrel to remove particles of metal or other foreign materials. If it is especially dirty you may want to follow with a solvent. This can then be wiped out with another cloth patch. Once it is clean, coat the inside of the barrel with a light film of gun oil on the wool ball. These wool oilers should be kept in clean, tightly closed containers free of foreign materials. They should last for several years. The outside metal parts of the gun can be easily cleaned by wiping them with a lightly oiled piece of wool, or a silicone-treated cloth obtainable in stores handling shooters' supplies. On the wooden parts of the gun ordinary furniture wax will work nicely, or you can obtain an inexpensive can of gunstock wax for the purpose.

How often should you clean a gun? This depends on two things: how you want it to look, and how much hard use you give it. Many shooters don't bother to clean the inside of the barrel from season to season. It is a good plan once in a while to break down an autoloader and clean all the metal parts that can be reached.

A shotgun should be inspected every time it comes in from the field. This does not mean that it needs another oiling, especially if it will be put to use again within a week or two. But it is a good idea to check its parts for moisture.

Some kinds of hunting, such as hunting grouse in thick-growing cover, shooting waterfowl in stormy weather, or hunting rails or ducks around salt water, are especially hard on guns. Salt-water spray can cause corrosion on metal parts unless proper care is taken to prevent it. A silicone-treated cloth offers protection.

At the end of a day around salt water, the outside metal parts should be wiped off with a moist cloth, then dried and lightly oiled. The in-

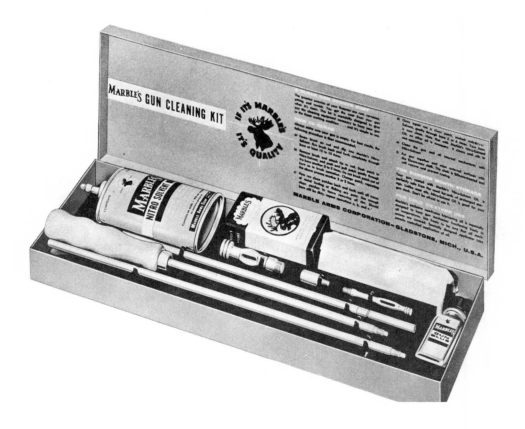

Gun cleaning kit useful in proper care of shotgun.
By Marble Arms Corp.

side of the barrel can be cleaned until dry, then oiled to prevent rust and corrosion.

One mistake often made in oiling a gun is oiling it too heavily. Too much oil can gum up the action, and also damage the stock. The best rule is to apply gun oils sparingly.

STORING YOUR SHOTGUN

When a shotgun is not in use the gun case protects it while traveling, and the gun cabinet while it is stored.

In some areas gun cases are required for transporting guns. In all areas they are desirable. They may be either simple canvas bags or fancy lined cases with special built-in protective edges and corners. Even the simplest case will protect a gun against scratches if it bounces around in the back of a car or pickup truck.

Left in the gun case over a period of weeks, the gun may collect moisture. The resulting rust may damage the metal parts seriously. Some gun cases have the inside treated for moisture protection.

The best gun cases, as far as protecting the gun in transit is concerned, are the rigid boxes made especially for the purpose and available in sporting goods and luggage stores. They are usually lined with a foam material to cushion the gun and hold it in place. Some cases are made to hold more than one gun. Metal-reinforced corners give them added rigidity.

For home storage of shotguns the shooter can employ either a gun cabinet or rack. The rack, especially the type holding guns in a horizontal position, has some advantages and some disadvantages. An open rack exposes guns to dust and dirt. On the other hand, in a dry room, the rack may be better than the air-tight gun cabinet.

Gun cabinets can be moisture-treated by keeping them equipped with a supply of moisture-absorbing silica gel. Some shooters equip gun cases with light bulbs. Turned on occasionally, a bulb can keep moisture down.

It is advisable to store guns and their ammunition in widely separated areas, or to lock the ammunition in a drawer. Some gun racks can be equipped with a crossbar that locks the guns to the rack.

Ammunition should always be stored where it will remain dry and cool. If it gets too hot it is likely to be ruined, and the moisture of a basement may damage it seriously.